D1075449

By Vinson Brown

THE AMATEUR NATURALIST'S HANDBOOK

HOW TO MAKE A HOME NATURE MUSEUM

HOW TO MAKE A MINIATURE ZOO

HOW TO UNDERSTAND ANIMAL TALK

HOW TO EXPLORE THE SECRET WORLDS
OF NATURE

HOW TO EXPLORE
THE SECRET WORLDS OF NATURE

HOW TO EXPLORE
The Secret Worlds of Nature

by Vinson Brown

Illustrated by Don Greame Kelley

Little, Brown and Company
Boston • Toronto

LIBRARY OF CONGRESS CATALOG CARD NO. 61-9280

THIRD PRINTING

Published simultaneously in Canada
by Little, Brown & Company (Canada) Limited

PRINTED IN THE UNITED STATES OF AMERICA

To my wife

BARBARA

who has inspired me with her love,

kindness, and constant help with my work

CONTENTS AND ILLUSTRATIONS

HOW TO EXPLORE
THE SECRET WORLDS OF NATURE

1

WHERE ARE THE SECRET WORLDS?

WOULD you like to stand like Columbus on the prow of a ship, and see before you a vast continent with new people and new animals and a thousand new flowers? The worlds that wait for discovery today are, mostly, smaller than the one Columbus found; but it is the attitude of the seeker and not the size of the discovery that brings the thrill to the explorer. Someday, somebody who reads these words may take off in a rocket ship for a distant planet, but there are discoveries to be made right here that are just as vital and full of meaning.

What is a secret world? It is an area of knowledge little known or penetrated by man. It may hide within itself all kinds of marvelous surprises — like the one that came to the old Dutch scientist Anton van Leeuwenhoek when he first looked through a microscope and saw the swarming microscopic life of a drop of pond water. Or the wonderful surprise the French scientist Pasteur received when he discovered how still tinier creatures, bacteria, cause disease. Each of these discoveries was made by a man who had the courage and patience to enter, explore carefully, and watch a secret world, a new world as yet unpenetrated by man.

Where are the secret worlds?

First, there are the worlds of your own back yard, of your house, and of your immediate neighborhood. Your house may be invaded by insects, mice, rats, cats, bacteria, even plants. Your back yard is likely to have insects, worms, moles, gophers, birds, or other creatures who visit it or live in it — some active by day, some by night, many of whose lives have been only partially or not at all explored by scientists. One insect alone may have a dozen or more secret worlds about itself to explore. Nothing may be known about its responses under varying conditions of heat or cold. The amount and variety of food it eats in a year may be unknown, or how it reacts to all sorts of danger.

You think all this may be unimportant? Some insects destroy crops of food that are worth hundreds of thousands of dollars; other insects may save these same crops. Still others bring diseases that may cause death or sickness to many thousands of people. A small discovery by one explorer might end some of such destruction or misery.

Second, there are the secret worlds of the city and its parks. If you live in a city, you could explore the lives of the dogs in your city and find out the patterns of behavior that make them act as they do. Postmen and other people who deliver things to homes throughout the city could tell you how the dogs act in different parts of the city. Then, if you could discover why the dogs act in a certain way, you might uncover a secret that would help your city make better plans for handling its dog problems. This is only one among many such secret worlds.

What are the patterns of cat and rat travel in your city, and how do they affect human lives? Where do wild animals hide in your city park, and why and how? What happens to escaped wild animal pets in the city, and which kinds are most successful in staying alive, and how?

Third, there are the secret worlds of the countryside. If you live in the country, you can make a wonderful variety of explorations. Even if you come to the country only for a summer visit, there is still much you can explore. The barnyard of a farm is full of things to discover, such as the way pigs teach each other lessons, or the effect of human friendliness or indifference on the production of milk by cows or goats, or the nature of the war between the farm cats and the mice and rats and gophers they feed on.

In the wilder country outside the farm there are hundreds of other worlds, often untouched and unknown. What does a bird's song really do for a bird? In how many different ways do the birds of one kind build their nests, and why? Where and how do the lizards go in winter, and what is their temperature variation there and outside? What happens to the bark of a pine tree as the pine tree grows? What wild medicines does a raccoon use when it is sick or hurt, and how effective are they?

Fourth, there are the secret worlds of other states and countries, which perhaps you have never seen, and which maybe you will never visit, but which you can still explore with the aid of books, by correspondence, and by trading specimens with the people who live in them. You could learn about the zones of life in Peru and even get specimens from the sides of the Andes, for instance, by writing to people there. You could find out about the breeds of dogs in Addis Ababa, the capital of Abyssinia, and how they are used by the men who raise them, perhaps in ways that would be useful in your own state.

Fifth, there are many secret worlds under the ground. The great sciences of geology, paleontology and archaeology are based largely on underground exploration. There is also the study of life there, some of it in the ground itself and some in caves. In caves and mines, in cores of rock brought up by oil drillers, and even in things that are uncovered with pick and shovel near the surface of the ground, lie many earth secrets. Most termite and ant nests are underground. And exploring these underground towns and cities has in it the thrill of discovering a lost and hidden civilization. Life that is found in soil — particularly such creatures as the earthworm — helps or hinders the growth of plants. That is why a discovery in the soil may be worth a fortune to the farmers.

Sixth, there are the secret worlds under water. You can put a submarine window in the side of a pond and watch the play of life and death. Or you can peer under the seaweed on the rocks beside the sea and find there secrets no man has found before. If you become a skin diver, new worlds are opened for your exploration.

Seventh, there are the secret worlds of the atmosphere and stratosphere. How far and for how long is dust carried from the explosion of a volcano, and how does it affect the color of clouds? Could you send a message to another country in a balloon, by having it soar to great heights and then letting it be carried by the winds of the stratosphere? What are the reasons behind the making of different kinds of clouds, and how do clouds tell stories in the sky?

Eighth, there are the secret worlds of outer space, which we can explore by telescope and radio waves, by radar and spectroscope, by rocket and satellite. If you live near an observatory and show sincere interest, you may find astronomers who will help you decide what upper worlds to explore. The falling of meteors and meteoric dust, the rays of light from an approaching comet, the mysterious dark nebulae that throw black curtains across sections of space — these and many others are calling for new exploration.

You can explore if you have the attitude and the driving force of the true explorer. You must want so much to learn the truth about what you are exploring that you will keep seeking even if what you find turns out to be directly contrary to what you at first believed and what other people tell you. The history of science is full of paradoxes, and of the truth turning out to be exactly the opposite of what everybody thinks. For example, the world looks flat to us, but scientists have proved that it is round; the sun looks as though it circles around the earth, but the truth found by scientists is that the earth circles the sun.

You must develop the courage and determination to keep exploring even when you are faced with constant difficulties and disappointments. This is the big test of the real explorer. Weaklings and mere would-be explorers give up when the going gets tough, or when people laugh at them and ridicule them. Almost every human being feels a desire to quit in the face of difficulty, but the explorer recognizes that overcoming obstacles is the best possible training for success, and that once you really tackle a difficulty with good spirit and intelligence it often proves to be not so bad as you thought. And an insurmountable one can be bypassed, if you apply your brains to finding a new way to tackle the problem. Commander Perry tried many times to reach the North Pole, failing again and again. Each failure actually taught him much about overcoming the fierce ways of the Arctic, so that finally he went on to victory. Pasteur went through thousands of disappointing failures before he developed effective vaccines to fight disease. Furthermore, he was constantly ridiculed and laughed at, by other so-called "scientists" as well as by government officials. "Don't give up the search; never give up!" — this is the motto of the true explorer.

You must develop an open mind, so eager to find the truth that you will seek equally in all directions for your goal. It is not easy to have such an open mind, because so many of us have been emotionally conditioned to believe many things without real foundation. For example, suppose you were exploring the actual danger of snakes to man. If you had been raised in a family which believed that snakes are evil and should all be killed or avoided, it would be very difficult for you to study snakes with the open mind of the scientist because you would have been emotionally conditioned to believe all snakes are bad, a belief completely unrelated to the true facts.

Whatever you decide to explore, you will need to know as much as possible about what other people have done in the same field. Often a study of their explorations will show you mistakes to avoid, and will lead you to trails that proved rewarding to them as well as into unknown areas which they have not yet entered. Look up books, magazines and scientific papers in libraries that deal with the subject you are studying. Even if your neighborhood library is small, it can often order books for you from a larger county or state library, or even from the libraries of great universities. Study carefully the research of others; make notes on whatever you think is important.

Keep a healthy skepticism in your mind towards what you find other people have written and what even the greatest scientists say to you. Remember that it is human to make errors. Your own research and experimenting may show that even a famous scientist can be wrong. Many of the greatest medical scientists in the middle of the nineteenth century laughed scornfully at the few doctors who were trying to teach that diseases could be passed from one person to another by dirty hands and instruments. Now we know how terribly wrong the scoffers were. Hundreds of thousands of people died painful deaths because of their blindness. Test as carefully as you can what other people say, and remember that one or two tests usually are far from enough. The true explorer may test and seek through hundreds of experiments before he begins to think he is on the track of truth.

You must realize that there is no real end to your exploration. Darwin spent most of a lifetime studying the evolution of plants and animals, but he died knowing that he had made only a small beginning, that many hundreds of new discoveries would be made in his field, perhaps modifying or even completely changing his own work. The true scientist withholds judgment of the discoveries that come from his exploration, no matter how carefully or how long he has tested, studied and experimented. While he thinks he is right, he knows that it is always possible that he could have made mistakes, and that future discoverers may prove wrong part or even all of what he has reported. For this reason the real explorer and scientist never becomes a "knower": he does not find absolute truths, but only relative truths. The only thing he truly *knows* is how easy it is for him to be wrong!

Collect the best tools you can find or build for exploration. Books are most important tools because they give you background knowledge and help you identify species. Some books you need to carry with you in the field (many such are mentioned at the end of this book). Remember too that books may have mistakes in them; and that you may make mistakes in your interpretation of what you read.

Instruments such as microscopes, telescopes, barometers and thermometers are often useful tools in exploration. Here, unfortunately, quality is a matter of cost, and you may find that you cannot afford the high quality of instrument you may need to complete your exploration. If this is so, you may have to set your goal on something that can be reached with the instruments you can afford. As you read farther in this book you will find many specific suggestions about instruments.

A notebook in which you write down your observations is vital to exploration. Most of us think that writing notes about what we see is unpleasant work, and we often seek almost any excuse to avoid doing it. I should like to advise beginning explorers who find note-taking hard not to do it at first, but just to observe, and so wait until they become thoroughly interested in what they are exploring before writing anything about it. When you are really interested, you will suddenly realize one day that you can neither get much out of the exploration yourself nor pass on to others any important information until you have taken careful notes. Then the more you see your notes grow the more fun you will have. There are examples of what I mean by notes on pages 44, 56 and 71.

It will help you a great deal to become associated in a friendly way with some scientist who is doing work in or near the field you wish to explore. If you can do so courteously, without bothering him at his own work or taking up too much of his time, get him to suggest ways and means to carry out your project. Often such a man will be most happy to help you if you are really sincere.

Plan your exploration in advance as much as you can, but never feel you have to follow any rigid plan. For beginners, the simpler the project of exploration the better. Most of the projects suggested in this book are simple, because the more complex take years of research and a vast amount of training. You will see here, as you study the different ways of exploring suggested, just how simple plans are made and carried out.

On your way then, Explorer, into the secret worlds of nature! And may your search bring you many wonders, and great treasures of knowledge and experience.

2

SECRET WORLDS OF YOUR HOUSE AND BACK YARD

IN THE darkness of the night, listen! In the middle of a hot summer afternoon, listen! Watch and listen, like a good detective following a criminal, like an explorer meeting head hunters who would like to kill him. This alertness, this awareness of what is going on around you, is the mark of the explorer. Even in your own back yard, even in your own house, you will see and hear many things that other people do not hear. For in your back yard and in your house there are both large worlds and small worlds waiting for you to explore. First, let us talk about the large worlds.

INSECTS AND THEIR RELATIVES IN YOUR HOUSE

In the warm times of the year insects and spiders and centipedes and similar creatures invade your home. Some come later, too, to get away from the cold. Listen! You will hear the buzz of a fly and then the deeper buzz of a wasp. Put your ear near an attic window and you will probably hear the soft, scuttling noise of a spider moving along her web into the crack which holds her hidden den. Sometimes, unfortunately, you can put your ear to the wood of your house and hear the termites signaling each other by tapping the wood with their jaws. Down in the basement a centipede glides on his several dozen legs into a hole in the cement, with a sound like a whispered tapping.

Night and day there are adventures and tragedies going on inside your home. Ant scouts have been sent into the house from a hidden city somewhere in your garden. They also are explorers of a world strange to them, the world of the house, seeking food by the aid of smell. The lead scouts, like Daniel Boone venturing into the unknown, advance carefully, their feelers quivering, seeking and seeking, but always ready to turn and run if danger threatens.

A wasp falls into a spider's web and fights for its life in the sticky web, trying desperately to sting the spider when the enemy draws near, buzzing its warning and war cry, ready to fight but aware that death is near.

All these creatures present many wonderful opportunities for exploration. You can be sure that, if you explore deep enough, soon you will be exploring where no human being has gone before. You might try to find out about all the kinds of insects and their relatives that live in or invade your home — where they come from, why they come, what they eat, how they hunt food, how they escape their enemies, and many other questions. Some of these creatures you would classify as house dwellers, living all the time inside, others as house invaders, coming from outside into one house to find food or shelter, but going outside again. Others would simply be blunderers, creatures that come blundering into your house without meaning to.

This sort of exploration will require a great deal of note-taking, the classification of species from books and museums, and the making of graphs and maps: graphs, to show how frequently and where different creatures appear; and maps of the house, to show lines of invasion and the favorite hiding places of the house dwellers. Probably to begin with you would like to try a simpler exploration, such as taking just one house creature and finding out all you can about it.

Choose your own creature; do not let me do it for you. But for the sake of showing how you might go about it, I am going to take the house spider (Figure 1). The house spider is the enemy of the good housekeeper, who is constantly knocking down its webs with a broom wrapped in a damp cloth. It is most active at night, and

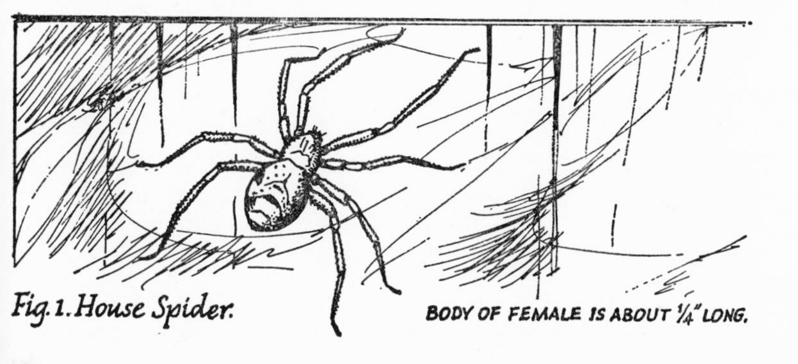

Fig. 1. House Spider.

you can find its trailing threads hanging from the ceiling the morning after. To you it is only a small gray spider that scuttles away in fright whenever you come near, but to the fly or small bug that it stalks across the wall, or traps in its web, it is a fearful tiger of the darkness, armed with poison-tipped jaws. To the ordinary person it is just a spider, to be stepped on or swatted and then forgotten, but to you it can be a special creature, leading you into its mysterious, secret world.

What do you want to find out about the house spider? Write down as many questions as you can think of, such as those that follow, and try to answer them through your exploration.

Where are the favorite hunting and hiding places of spiders in your house or outbuilding? Draw a map of each floor of the building (Figure 2), and mark on the map all the webs you find and where they are, numbering each web. Use a different colored ink or pencil to mark on the map any new webs you find each day. Put the numbers at the bottom of the map, and after each number the date when first seen and the date when last seen. Mark also the trailing streamers left by the spiders at night. Gradually you will come to know intimately where the spiders are found, and where they like to go. This knowledge will help you with much of your other exploration into the life of the house spider.

What does the spider fear and how does it try to escape from danger? This is one of numerous questions that can be answered only by careful and patient watching. Try to see the spider under every possible condition. You may have to tease it out of its nest to see how it acts

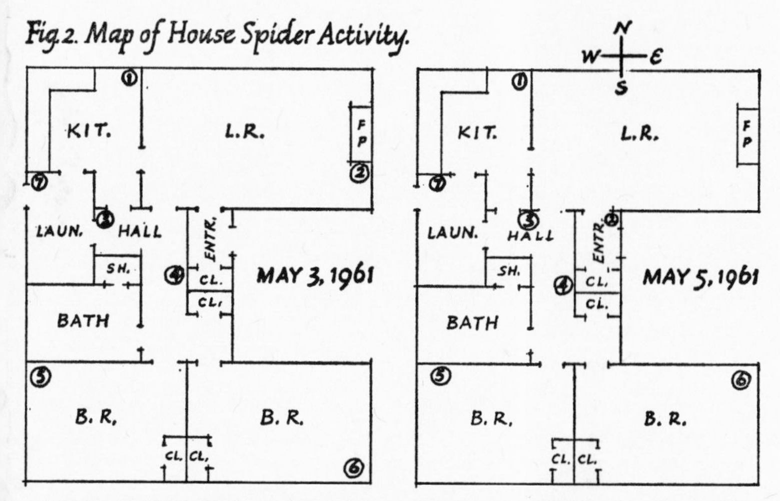

Fig. 2. Map of House Spider Activity.

1. LARGE SPIDER, PROBABLY FEMALE. PERMANENT PLACE UP IN HIGH N.E. CORNER. 10 FLIES OBSERVED IN WEB.
2. SMALL MALE SPIDER. DISAPPEARED ON MAY 5. ONLY FRAGMENT OF WEB LEFT. 2 FLIES CAUGHT.

3-7. INFORMATION ON OTHER SPIDERS AS ABOVE.

in the open. You will probably find it is terrified to be away from its hiding place in the daylight, but will come out at night when the darkness gives it protection from enemies. If you use a red flashlight at night, you will find that the red light rarely disturbs the spider as a white light would, and you can watch while moving about naturally, as long as you move with the utmost quietness. Try putting different insects in the spider's web, finding out which ones it is afraid of and why, and which it attacks without hesitation.

Another question you might ask is whether a spider can be trained? Of course you have heard about trained fleas; so why not a trained spider? Most animals can be trained with rewards of food. You can touch your spider's web with a light brush, and then feed it a fly. Keep this up until it is used to coming for its fly dinner every time you touch the web once lightly with the brush. After a while try touching the web twice and giving the spider a wasp or a large ant. It may have one reaction for one touch and an entirely different reaction for two. You have begun to train it. Perhaps you can go on from this and teach it to come when called, or to hide when a certain word is given, and even other tricks. What is the good of this? Well, for one thing, it helps you understand your spider better, for another it could lead to the training of an animal that might be useful in some special way to man.

A question of real and vital importance is whether the house spider is of economic benefit to mankind and whether this benefit outweighs the trouble it gives the housekeeper? You will have to do some hard but exciting exploration to find the answer to this. Two insects the house spider catches and eats that are often very harmful to man, are the house fly and the mosquito. Every time a house spider kills one of these insects which may carry a dangerous disease like typhoid or yellow fever, it may either be saving a human life or at least preventing a serious and expensive sickness. If one house spider during its entire life killed enough flies to prevent one person from being sick in bed for two weeks, that one spider would be worth at least a hundred dollars and probably a lot more to the person saved. We can be pretty sure that one hundred dollars would be more than worth the trouble one spider could give a housekeeper.

It is difficult to put a definite figure like this on the value of any one house spider, but if you did enough research and exploration you could probably make a pretty accurate guess. You could find out from the Department of Public Health in your city or county what proportion of house flies and mosquitoes they believe from their studies carry disease. Then you could watch say ten house spiders and find out how many flies and mosquitoes those spiders killed and ate during one month. If the house spiders killed and ate 250 flies and mosquitoes in a month, the average per spider would be twenty-five. If the health authorities told you one out of every twenty-five mosquitoes and flies carried a bad disease, you could say that each of those spiders was far more valuable than it was harmful around the house.

These are only a few samples of questions you could ask about the house spider and stories of how you could find their answers. Whatever secret world of the house you decide to explore, whether insect or spider, mouse or house-loving bird, ask as many questions as you can and then explore and explore until you can answer them.

LIFE IN YOUR BACK YARD

Your back yard usually contains insects, worms, spiders, moles, gophers, birds and other creatures who visit it or live in it, some active by day, some by night. Many of them have been only partially or not at all explored by scientists. One insect alone may have a dozen or more unknown facts about itself for you to explore. Nothing may be known about its response or activity under varying conditions of heat or cold. How it reacts to danger, or the amount and variety of food it eats in a year may be unknown. Knowledge of its food may be particularly important, for some insects destroy crops of food that are worth hundreds of thousands of dollars. Other insects may save these same crops. Still other insects bring diseases to many thousands of people. A small discovery by one real explorer may end destruction or misery.

Another true adventure can always be found in exploring the life of a bird. Your back yard should be a happy place for birds to come to. Supply them with a bathing place (one that is safe from cats), food stands, and food in winter when food is scarce, bushes and vines in which to hide. Some berry bushes, such as hawthornes and toyon, are particularly attractive to birds and bring in many species. (See my book, *How to Make a Miniature Zoo.*) You can, of course, study all the birds that visit or live in your back yard to find out why they come, and how they live while there, but perhaps it would be best at first to choose one bird and study it carefully.

When I was a boy on a ranch in the country I had the greatest fun studying the life of a barn owl. The barn owl sometimes comes into back yards in cities and nests in outbuildings — so I want to tell you what I did, also what I could have done if I had known then how to be a real explorer.

My first experience with the barn owl was a tragic one. I had my first twenty-two rifle that summer, and I was very proud of it. I shot some animals that were good to

Fig. 3.

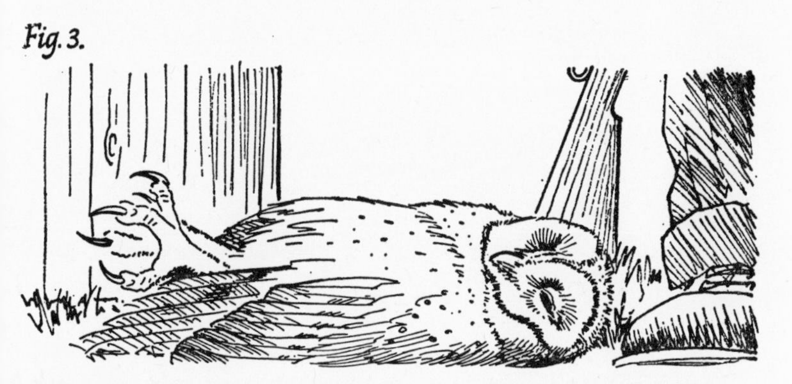

shoot, such as rats and ground squirrels, which do a lot of harm to the farmer's crops. But one day I stood with my gun under a big palm tree and heard a strange rustling among the thick leaves.

Looking up, I saw a queer monkeylike face peering down at me. The leaves were so thick that I could not see the rest of the creature, but that face, with its big yellow eyes, frightened me, and I raised my gun and fired at it. A weird scream answered the sound of the shot, and down to the ground plummeted a white and brown body. When it fell at my feet I saw it was an owl. The sharp beak clicked together twice, as the poor bird tried to strike at the enemy that had hurt it, then I saw the light fade out of those beautiful yellow eyes.

I felt very sad at the death of the big bird, but still I was excited over my kill and did not know just what it was. I took the dead bird to a gardener who knew and loved birds and asked him what it was. I saw shock and anger come over his brown face.

"Boy!" he said. "Do you know that you have killed the

most valuable friend of the rancher and farmer? This is a barn owl, and barn owls kill and eat their weight in harmful mice and rats every few days. You should never kill such a bird. If the government of the state found out what you have done, they would fine you fifty dollars for your mistake."

I shall always remember how sternly he looked at me and how sick at heart I was at what I had done. Never again did I shoot at a bird or animal that I knew was a friend of man. But not long after the tragedy of the shooting, which was probably not only a tragedy for the adult owl, but also for her young, I started to study other barn owls. There was a big barn on the ranch, and high up in one end mother and father barn owl had made an untidy nest of feathers and straw in which were laid five large white eggs.

I discovered this nest one evening when I stood under the end of the barn and heard a strange ghost-like snoring and hissing noise above my head. My heart suddenly took a jump when what looked like a real ghost soared out from the top of the barn on absolutely soundless wings. The owl swept away into the gathering darkness, probably on a hunting trip. I took a flashlight up into the great dark barn and there, high in the far end where the cobwebs hung like dark clusters of lichen, I found the nest. The adults were both gone hunting, so I looked very closely at the eggs and found them to be pure white and about two and a half inches long.

The next day I came back and found one of the big birds standing guard over the nest. As I approached it began a most peculiar dance, lifting first one foot and then the other, fluffing out its feathers, hunching its shoulders and thrusting its head toward me fiercely. When I came still closer the sharp bill began to clack together sharply and warningly. At that point I stopped and sat very still, watching the barn owl for a long time. The great yellow eyes glared straight at me, but gradually the bill stopped clacking and the feet stopped moving.

When the owl's mate came winging in through the opening in the top of the barn, it did not see me at first, but it became quickly aware there was danger near when it saw the puffed out feathers of its mate. Now two monkeylike faces stared at me and two pairs of great yellow eyes glared at me fiercely.

During the next few days I came several times to see my barn owls. It was a great thrill to watch the baby birds break out of their shells. The fluffy bits of white seemed to be almost all mouth. Into these gaping mouths the adults plumped mouse after mouse. One time I counted no less than thirteen mice going down one baby's throat. Gradually, the mother and father came to accept me as not dangerous to their young, though every so often a bright yellow eye would look to see what I was up to.

Very early I noticed a strange thing about these owls. In the evening, after they had brought in and eaten most of the mice that were caught, they would fly out for a minute to a perch on the wall of the building, and make queer twisting movements with their necks. What in the world are they doing? I wondered. For a long time I could not figure it out. Then one evening I went down to the ground below and waited. Soon a barn owl appeared on the perch and twisted its neck about. Suddenly, "plop" — something wet landed on the ground near my feet. Turning on my flashlight I found what I had entirely missed before, a pile of gray, furry pellets, each from around an inch to two inches long. When I examined these I found that they were full of the fur, teeth and bones of mice and other small creatures that had been killed and then swallowed by the owls. But not all had stayed down. The indigestible parts were thrown up and spit out. And the owls did this several times every day!

You can see that I was rapidly learning a lot about them, but one thing was missing. This was a knowledge of how to explore secret worlds. I was very close to the edge of such a world, but no one had ever shown me

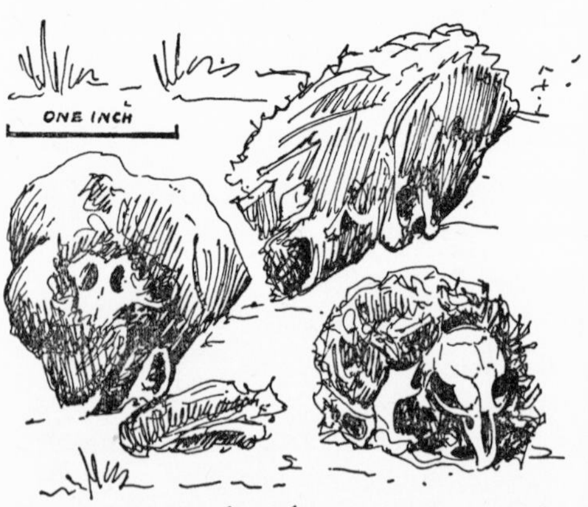

DR. A.K. FISHER REPORTED THAT 200 PELLETS COLLECTED FROM BENEATH THE NEST OF A PAIR OF BARN OWLS IN A TOWER OF THE SMITHSONIAN BUILDING, WASHINGTON, D.C., CONTAINED 454 SKULLS: 225 MEADOW MICE; 2 PINE MICE; 179 HOUSE MICE; 20 RATS; 6 JUMPING MICE; 20 SHREWS; 1 STAR-NOSED MOLE; 1 VESPER SPARROW. (BENT: *LIFE HISTORIES OF NORTH AMERICAN BIRDS OF PREY, PART 2.* U.S. NAT. MUS. BULLETIN 170, 1938. PAGE 146)

Fig. 4. Barn Owl Pellets on the Ground Beneath a Nest—Proof of the value of these birds in controlling harmful rodents.

how to enter it. I needed to ask myself questions — lots of questions — and to then try to find the answers, patiently, carefully, intelligently, and with enthusiasm.

What questions should I have asked? Well, what about those mysterious pellets of fur that I had found on the ground below the barn? I could have asked, What messages do they tell? Then I could have collected hundreds of them, and, if I had studied them carefully, they would have told me just what kinds of animals the barn owls caught and what percentage of their diet each kind was. Instead of a lot of guesswork, I could have found out exactly how much value the barn owls were to man, for I could have found out the number and kinds of harmful rodents two barn owls destroyed in a given time. Of course this would have taken some real detective work. I would have had to take the different kinds of bones I found to scientists to get them to help me identify the different kinds of animals those bones represented. The nearest university, college or museum would have been a good place to go.

Another interesting question would have been, How do the owls communicate or talk with each other? I had listened to their strange snoring and hissing, but I had not tried to understand how to divide these sounds up into different meanings; nor had I understood, except vaguely, that the owls were really talking together, and to me, by their movements and the expressions in their eyes. The fluffing out of the feathers, for example, was a warning to me not to come closer, as was the strange dance and the hunching of the shoulders. But really to understand these mysterious creatures I needed to watch them with my eyes alert for even slight movements or expressions. My ears needed to be ready to catch the tiniest sound. Gradually I needed to feel such kinship to them that I would begin to feel like an owl; and suddenly one day or evening, as has happened to me with other animals, I would really begin to understand them. Like most animals, owls can transfer to each other in the flash of a second complete understanding and feelings that might take a man several sentences to express.

A third vital question would be, How do barn owls train their children? Most young birds instinctively know what to do or what to say when they are hungry or in danger or wish to fly. But there are always some things their parents must teach them to help them survive in a cruel and dangerous world. As the little owls grew older I saw them copying their parents. They too would hiss and snore a shriller warning and fluff out their feathers if they thought that danger was coming near. Later came the great day of the first attempts at flight. First they tried flying in the barn itself. These were very short and clumsy attempts, sometimes landing almost upside down, but what fun when they did it right! And the parents encouraged and cheered them on by hissing at them gently and by themselves flying about in short flights to show how it was done. Unfortunately I could not wait long enough to see how the father and mother owl would teach their young to take the great adventure of flying out of the barn. Really to answer the question about training I would have had to follow them into the woods, watching carefully to see how the adults taught the young ones to hunt for food.

There are other questions and other explorations you can make into the life of any bird, but these will give you some idea of how you might start exploring one secret world in your back yard.

Some of the innumerable kinds of ants in the world are bound to be building their cities in your backyard. Ants are restless folk, always on the move except when the cold of winter drives them to hide and sleep deep under the ground. To study them and their city is so much like visiting and watching a city of tiny human beings that sometimes you think you can put your ear down and hear the gossip when two ants meet! Certainly they seem to be talking together, often very seriously, and sometimes they run excitedly when the message seems to be urgent.

I have explored many ant cities, but perhaps the most interesting was the enormous one of the red leaf-cutting ants in Panama. The first part of my exploration was to watch the ants on the surface of the ground. They had long lines of workers extending out for many yards in several directions from the main entranceways. Each line had two columns — one column of ants going out into the field to bring back leaf pieces, and the other column carrying the pieces of cut leaves back to the nest. There were three kinds of red workers: large, medium and small. When I walked out to the bush which they were stripping of leaves, I found that the small and medium-sized ants did most of the cutting of the leaves with their sharp jaws, while the large size workers carried the leaf pieces back to the city. The line of ants carrying leaf

Fig. 5. Leaf-cutting Ants (Genera: ATTA, ACROMYRMEX)

pieces looked like a line of small sailboats with green sails. Sometimes the tiniest workers even hitchhiked rides home by riding on the tops of the green sails!

Some ants were sent out as scouts to find new bushes or trees they could strip of leaves. They moved clumsily over the land, looking and looking. When they found a bush or tree they liked, they laid a scent trail back to the city so that other ants could follow this to the plant. I was anxious to test the intelligence of the ants, so I dug a deep trench across one of the ant pathways. Then I put a bridge across the trench. To my amusement the ants did not use the bridge, but insisted on climbing down and up the sides of the trench to reach the other side. However, the next morning, when I came again, there they were streaming confidently across the little bridge! I wish I had found the answer to the question of how, why and when they started using that bridge.

The next day I took shovel and pick and started digging down into the ant city. Immediately out of the holes rushed the soldier ants to attack me. These were big red ants nearly an inch long with enormous heads and jaws. They could give a painful bite, but they were also very clumsy, so I protected my legs with leggings and brushed the ants off as fast as they tried to climb up to attack me. One, however, managed to get past my guard, because I suddenly felt a burning pain on the back of my neck!

Three or four feet down I began to run into large underground rooms, some more than a foot long, as big to the ants as hundred-foot-long halls are to us. In these rooms were the most fantastic gardens I have ever seen, gardens of a kind of yellowish fungi (related to mushrooms) that were being cultivated by the ants just as men cultivate vegetable gardens. These fungus gardens were growing on a mulch made of the pieces of leaves that the ants brought from above ground. It was a wonderful way to keep themselves well supplied with food.

At six feet down I found one of the queens in a six-inch chamber. She was surrounded by rows of ferocious-looking guards who immediately rushed to attack me, while smaller nurse ants scurried about her in great alarm. She was a fat and rather ugly-looking queen, far larger than her helpers, and she was laying eggs as fast as the nurse ants could carry them off to hide in special nursery rooms in other parts of the underground city.

If you think I was the only enemy attacking that city, you are wrong. I saw ants of different species, so tiny they were hardly more than microscopic, who had made minute tunnels in the walls of the big ants' rooms. They had stolen fungus food from the leaf-carrying ants and carried it away to special hiding places. There were also rove-beetles, who looked a lot like the regular red leaf-carrying ants, and must have smelled like them too, because the guards of the ant city left these beetles alone.

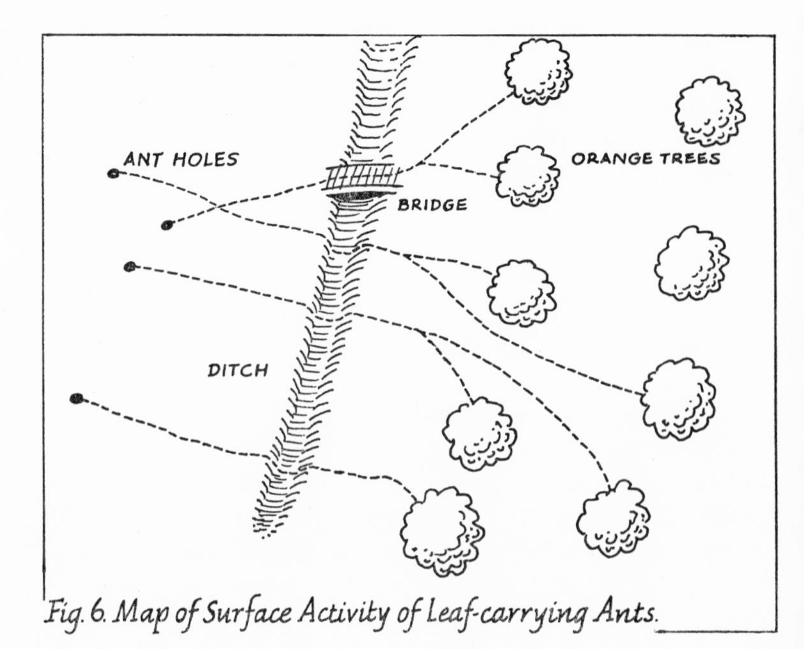

Fig. 6. Map of Surface Activity of Leaf-carrying Ants.

But what sly spies and pirates they were! I watched one of these beetles lying in wait along one of the ant passageways. It sprang out at a passing ant and sank its powerful jaws into the ant's head. There was a short, fierce struggle, and the ant was dead — and soon eaten. Many such parasites and killers infested that great city.

To record what I had learned about the ant city I first made a map of the surface activity of the city, showing the location of the entranceways and then the trails that led to different bushes and trees (as you can see in Figure 6). Then I drew a cross-section map of the city as I had dug into it, for I had dug a pit with straight-up-and-down sides in order to show what scientists call a "profile." This profile is shown in the second map (Figure 7). On this map I marked the fungus chambers, the queen's room, the nursery rooms and other underground rooms. I also showed where I had found parasites and other ant enemies, and the underground guests of the ant city. Later I made several maps of the city at different levels. (Figure 8). However, the leaf-carrying ant city I had dug into probably covered several hundred and possibly even thousands of square yards of ground, and would have taken a whole army of careful diggers to map completely and correctly. Any ant city you might find in your back yard would probably be much smaller.

Many secrets are hidden in these cities. Here are a few of the questions I asked myself in exploring that secret world of the ants:

(1) What leaves did the ants prefer and why? They seemed to prefer orange-tree leaves, so much so that we had to put poison around the trunks of our orange trees

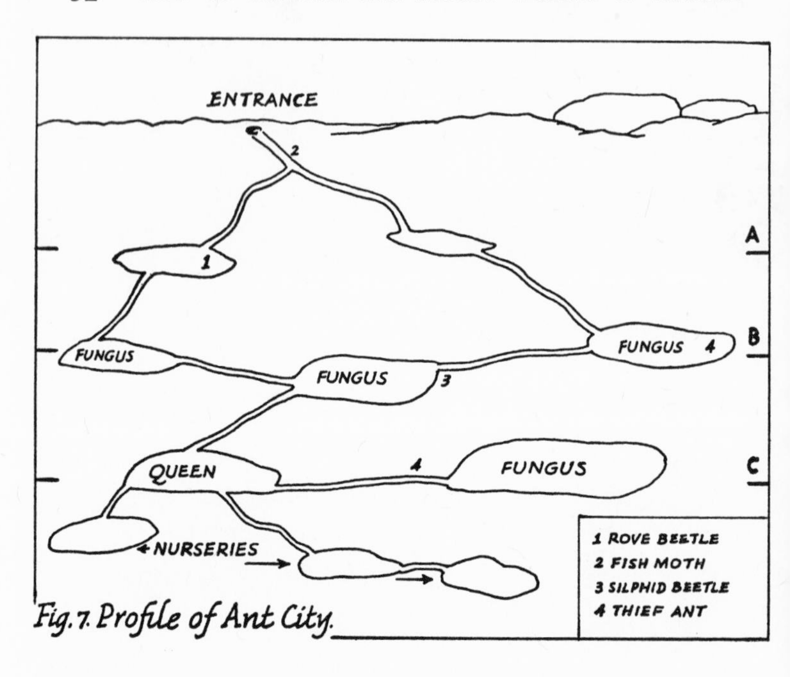

Fig. 7. Profile of Ant City.

to keep the trees from being killed. Probably the ants liked them because they formed a better mulch than other leaves for the underground fungus gardens to grow on, but to be sure of this I would have had to raise some of the fungus on different kinds of leaf mulch, and then test the ants to see which of several different fungus gardens they preferred the taste of. Still I think there is little doubt the orange leaves gave a flavor to the fungus that the ants liked.

(2) Were the soldier ants commanded by officers? In other words, did they fight against an enemy in an organ-

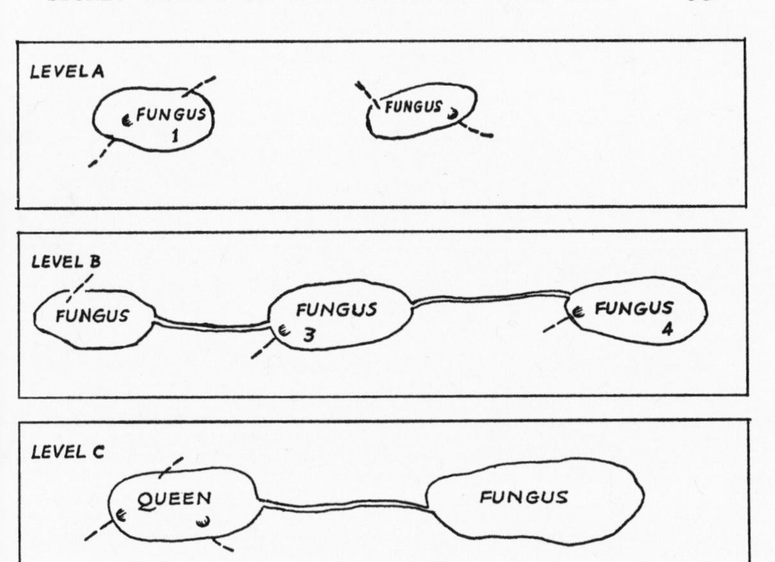

Fig. 8. Cross-section Plans of Ant City.

ized way, or did they just fight as individuals? I watched the big red soldiers very carefully, and saw that whenever I opened up a new tunnel the soldiers rushed up through the hole to attack me, while the smaller ants retreated below. The soldiers seemed to come with a concerted rush, as if they had been given a signal by someone, but when they got to the surface, they spread out, helter-skelter, in all directions, looking for the enemy. When they found my shoes and leggings, they immediately tried to bite. My observations seemed to show that, while they came out in a rush, as if on order, once they started attacking it was pretty much an individual fight. There were certainly no clearly marked squads of soldiers under command of officers.

(3) Did the ants have any plan or method for attacking and driving out the parasites and robbers who infested their city? We know that in human cities we have police who protect honest citizens against robbers and other criminals. However, in all my watching of the city of the leaf-carrying ants, I saw no sign of such a police force for ants. There was, of course, the army of soldiers who fought against invaders from outside, but I could see no evidence that these soldiers also acted against an inner enemy. This does not necessarily mean that the ants had no way to fight their inner enemies. My week's observation of their city was not nearly long enough in time to show conclusive evidence one way or the other.

There are, of course, many other questions you can try to answer by exploring your ant or termite city. Be sure to ask all the questions you can think of.

A few other worlds you might explore in your back yard include:

(1) The snails and slugs — where and how they hide and what they like to eat most.

(2) The pathways of lizards — how and where and why they use them most.

(3) The wild plants — how they reproduce themselves and successfully spread their kinds.

(4) The leaves of trees and bushes — their relative size and shape in relation to the amount of sunlight and shade they get each day.

(5) The hunting methods of ground beetles — the number of pests they eliminate on the average each night.

(6) The hunting methods of wasps — and their success.

MICROSCOPIC WORLDS

If you have a good microscope, you have a tool for exploration that can lead you into many secret worlds even when your house is blanketed with snow and the cold winds of a blizzard blow outside. Most young people, when they are given a microscope, use it with great interest for a few days, then put it away in some back closet where it may uselessly gather dust for years. Perhaps if you earn the money for a microscope you will appreciate it more than if it is given to you. One reason for losing interest in a microscope may be that it has poor optics and is hard to handle accurately. If this is so, then put such a microscope aside right now and start saving your money for a good secondhand one or new one.

In buying a microscope it is best to get the advice of someone who has handled many of them, such as a biology teacher or professor or a doctor, who can tell you what to look for in your machine. Above all, optical clarity and easy mechanical handling are essential. It is best to get one also that has at least three different lenses for different magnifications. One magnification should be at least 250 times for looking at very small things. For studying insect body parts a magnification of 25 times is good.

You can quickly become bored with even a good microscope if you look through it only for fun and idle curiosity. It is necessary to have a purpose behind your looking. A good purpose and the fighting courage and stick-to-it-iveness to achieve it are the two vital ingredients in microscope study.

I am going to suggest some purposes to you, but there are a number of other sources you can turn to for suggestions. In the back pages of *Natural History Magazine* many suggestions can be found about the microscope and its uses. There are also good books (such as those listed at the end of this book) that tell you about various microscope projects. Obtain these from your library. There are also societies of microscopists who can help you (these, too, are listed at the end of this book).

The simplest way to get some microscopic plants and animals to study is to take water from an old fish pond, including some of the scum and algae you find in it, and put bits of this on your microscope slides. Another way is to gather dried-up weeds, grass and other plants, or bits of hay, and put them in a jar full of water. Allow it to stand several days where some sunlight, but not too much, can reach it, and you will soon have all kinds of microscopic things to watch.

Most beginners take a drop of water from a pond and put this unprotected on a slide. The trouble with this is that the drop soon dries up. It is best to form a circle or square of glue or clear cement in the middle of the slide about an eighth of an inch high and allow this to dry. After the glue or cement or balsam is dry, take an eyedropper and drop your water for study into the little hollow that has been formed. Then cover this over with a very thin square or round piece of glass, called a "cover glass", that will hold the water in place and prevent it from evaporating. You will thus be able to study the same drop for many hours (Figure 9).

Following are a few projects that can give you real purpose in studying the life in water through the microscope:

(1) Take one kind of plant or animal to the microscope and watch it carefully. (This kind of observation has always brought to human knowledge remarkable

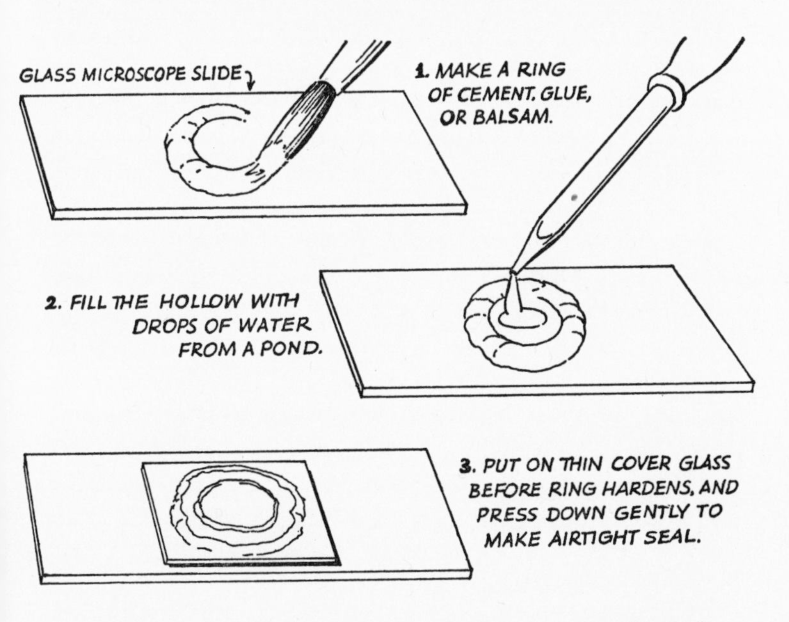

Fig. 9. Preparing Microscope Slide for Study of Pond Water Life.

new discoveries. For example, in bacteriological laboratories all over the world scientists are doing concentrated study of individual organisms, finding out truths that may be used in fighting human disease or in adding to human health, homes and industries. But there are so many hundreds of thousands of different kinds of microscopic life that the scientists have time for intensive study of only comparatively few. It is always possible that you may, by carefully studying something they have not yet studied, find new facts of importance.) Suppose you plan to study a species of *Euglena* (Figure 10), which is a very peculiar little creature that seems to be half plant, half animal — because it has within its cell the green chlorophyll that is used by plants to manufacture food, yet can swim about freely like an animal. You will first need to identify your kind of Euglena from a book (such as one of those mentioned at the end of this book), and then double-check your own identification by taking some examples of the animal to show a scientist who is a specialist on microscopic life, or sending slides of them to him for iden-

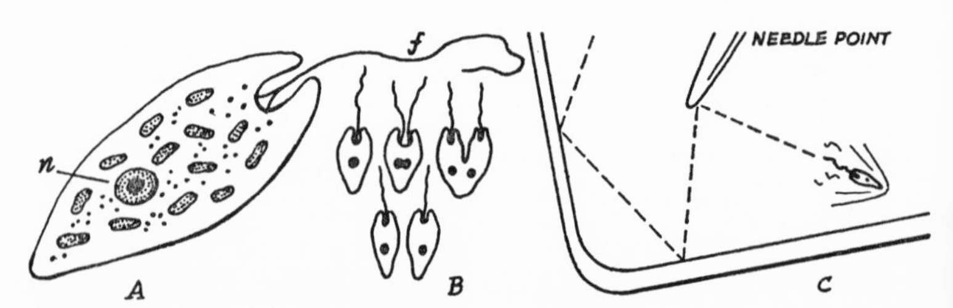

Fig. 10. *Euglena*, a Protozoan: (A) GREATLY ENLARGED TO SHOW NUCLEUS (*n*), FLAGELLUM (*f*), AND OTHER PARTS; (B) STEPS IN DIVISION; (C) MOVEMENTS, SHOWING TENDENCY TO GO IN STRAIGHT LINE.

tification. How to prepare stained slides of microscopic animals is a complex job that is described in books on microscopic technique. After you have found exactly what species of Euglena you are watching, you need to write that name into your notebook and start taking notes about everything you see the creature do. Here are a few of the questions you will try to answer, through observation and experimentation: What does the Euglena eat and how does it eat? How does it get rid of waste products such as carbon dioxide and indigestible parts of food? What enemies does it have and how do they attack it? What does the Euglena do in its own defense? How long does the average Euglena live, and what are the signs that it is nearing the end of its life? How does the body, both inside and outside, of a Euglena change as it gets older? How does it reproduce its own kind? What unusual or significant actions can you find the Euglena doing and how and why is it doing them?

Remember that patient and careful attention to details is the great key to success in finding secrets of real value. The person who gets discouraged easily or does not take the time for thorough observation ends with little information worth talking about.

(2) Study a food chain. By a food chain, scientists mean the chain of animals and plants that eat one another. Thus a microscopic plant is eaten by a paramecium, the paramecium is eaten by a rotifer or wheel animalcule, the wheel animalcule is eaten by a small fish. The small fish is eaten by a large fish. The large fish is caught and eaten by a man. (See Figure 11.) Such a food chain includes both microscopic and larger life.

Fig. 11. A Food Chain: FROM ONE-CELLED PLANT TO PARAMECIUM TO ROTIFER TO SMALL FISH TO LARGE FISH TO MAN.

You study the food chain partly with a microscope and partly with your eyes. The main thing is to find the effect of these different organisms on each other in the "balance" of nature. "Balance" means that no particular creature is allowed to become so numerous or so scarce that it breaks this chain. Just how the balance is maintained is a secret for you to find out.

(3) Find out how a certain animal or animals are influenced by changes in their environment. You can measure a small amount of salt into the water in which your microscopic animals are living and see how this affects them and what percentage of salt each kind will stand. This is called its "margin of survival." Other chemicals, such as iodine, soda, acid, and so on, can be added in measured quantities and the animals tested. Be sure you know the exact proportion of chemical to water, and keep this in your records. You can also change the nature of the environment by increasing or decreasing the amount of sunlight received each day, or the amount of mud in the water, or the amount of plants. Keep careful records of all the changes noted. Often these changes can be drawn on a graph.

(4) Still other secret worlds to explore include: (*a*) the relationship of algae in pond water to the amount of sunlight the pond receives; (*b*) the effect of currents on different kinds of microscopic life; (*c*) the different ways algae reproduce themselves; (*d*) the different speeds of an ameba in water, particularly its speed when disturbed; (*e*) a study of the different ways microscopic life protects itself against drying up. And so on.

Besides looking at microscopic life in water, you can watch for it also in human and animal blood. You can watch the living blood in action in the thin membrane of a frog's foot if you put the frog to sleep — carefully — with chloroform and put the foot under the microscope so you can look at the membrane between the toes. (NOTE: This should be done only under the supervision of a science teacher or experienced adult.)

Then there is the fascinating study of skin and body sections of animals and plants when cut into thin sections by a microscope section knife. These sections are glued to a microscope slide with clear balsam and covered with a thin square of glass. (As we saw in Figure 9.) If you do not have your own section knife, perhaps you can have sections made for you at a biology laboratory. Sections are studied carefully to find out the size and shape of all the inner organs of a plant or animal body. From this study three-dimensional wax or rubber models can be made of the different organs, or even of cross-sections of the body. (For details on how to make wax and rubber models, see my book called *How to Make a Home Nature Museum*.) Among the many secret worlds to be explored with these methods is how a particular animal or plant uses its inner organs and how these organs are particularly adapted for its needs.

This chapter has presented only a few suggestions about the secret worlds of your back yard and home. From books and from scientists you can find hundreds of others to explore.

3

SECRET WORLDS
OF THE CITY AND ITS PARKS

NIGHT and day there comes the roar of a great city. Far into the night trucks and cars still dash along the lighted streets. The clang, the smoke, the noise often seem endless, but hidden under the surface noise and the busy movement of thousands of people the secret worlds of nature await the explorer. These worlds, of course, are found most often in the parks where bushes and trees grow and there are stretches of green grass and rippling water. But even in the dingier parts of the city, wherever there is the least sign of animal and plant life there are secret worlds. Let us look first at the city, as separate from its parks.

AMONG STREETS AND BUILDINGS

One of the great wars going on in any city has man and cat on one side and rats and mice on the other. Through the dark sewers, through holes in the walls, in hiding places behind piles of boxes and sacks and cans full of food or fuel, the rats and mice move on their secretive ways, eating food, destroying goods — always destroying. Through the shadows comes the cat — usually a scrawny alley cat, but sometimes a cat placed in the building by the owner. The cat crouches in darkness and moves on feet as soft as velvet. Its tail-tip twitches as it waits in long patience by a hole. Suddenly it jumps and a big rat squeaks in fear and rage. Sharp claws and teeth sink in, and the rat is shaken viciously while the cat growls its warning that this is its food.

You have just seen a secret world you might further explore, but unless you are very sharp of eye and mind you probably missed most of it. Just how did that cat kill that rat?

Cats use different methods — some more effective than others, some in which the claws are more important than the teeth and some the other way around. If you could study the catching and killing methods of as many cats as possible, you might find that one cat had developed a far more successful way than others. Perhaps you could raise from this cat a breed of cats that would be of immense value to man in catching mice and rats. But such a project would mean long study, much note-taking and observation, and finally careful experimentation and breeding.

Why not make a careful, over-all study of the fierce war of the cats against the mice and rats? Does the situation change? Do the mice and rats sometimes have the best of it, and sometimes the cats? Have the rats ever ganged up on a cat as the baboons of Africa sometimes gang up on a leopard? Have cats ever hunted mice or rats in a pack, as a pack or pride of lions in Africa sometimes hunts antelope? Have mice and rats developed new ways to avoid cats or to trick them? Have the cats developed new ways to catch mice and rats? Where are the favorite hunting places of the cats? Where are the favorite hiding places of the rats and mice, and why do they go there? You can perhaps map out the places where these animals stay and their usual routes of travel in your neighborhood. (See Figure 12.)

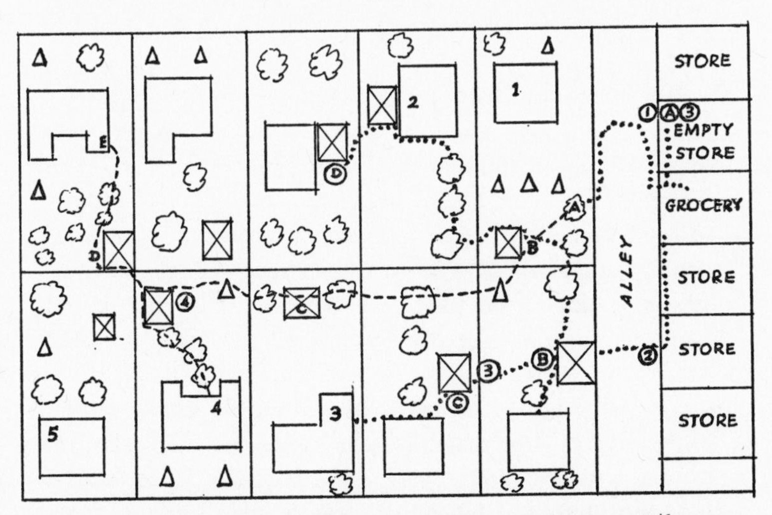

Fig. 12. Map of City Block Showing Cat, Rat, and Mouse Hideouts.

DECIDUOUS TREES ◯ — CATS-HUNTING ①, ②, ETC.,–RESTING 1, 2, ETC.
CONIFEROUS TREES Δ — RATS-HIDEOUTS Ⓐ, Ⓑ, ETC.,–RUNWAYS ••••••
OUTBUILDINGS ⊠ — MICE-HIDEOUTS A, B, ETC.,–RUNWAYS ----

"NATURE-DETECTING"

Let us consider briefly and in outline a crime that Sherlock Holmes solved, called "The Case of Black Peter." Black Peter was the retired captain of a seal-hunting ship, who was found killed by his own sealing harpoon in a cabin on his estate. The police caught a man a week later breaking into the cabin to look for some papers of Black Peter, and accused him of the crime when they found he had good reason to seek revenge: Black Peter, years before, had killed the man's father and stolen valuables from him. To the police it seemed an open-and-shut case.

But Sherlock Holmes was not so sure. He had the imagination to see that the crime could have been done by somebody else. He had made a very patient and careful search of its scene and found at least two things that showed that somebody else was probably the true murderer. One of these was an old leather sealer's tobacco pouch, which could have been Black Peter's because it had his initials on it, but probably was not because Black Peter did not smoke. The other fact was that Black Peter was a big, powerful man, and yet the harpoon that killed him had been driven clear through his body and into the wall behind. This made it likely that a very powerful man had killed Black Peter, while the man accused of the crime was small and of only moderate strength.

Sherlock Holmes, carrying out his thorough methods of investigation, went to a neighborhood butchershop and tried running a spear through the body of a dead pig. He found that, strong as he himself was, it was almost impossible to run the body clear through. He then advertised in the newspaper for a harpooner to go on a sealing expedition, and, when men came to apply for the job, had the police officer who was working on the case present for the interviews. One of the harpooners was a large and very strong man. He was trapped by Sherlock Holmes into admitting that he was the man who had killed Black Peter when Black Peter tried to kill him, and the case was solved.

Notice that the tendency of the English police in this case was to seek a quick and easy solution. Once they found one man who, they thought, could be the criminal, they stopped searching. They were not being scientific; they were making a terrible mistake. The true explorer of secret worlds must be like Sherlock Holmes in his exploration and not like the police in this particular case. It is human and very easy to be misled by surface evidence into coming to a premature and wrong conclusion.

Suppose you find on your street or nearby a tree that seems to be gradually dying, so you start out to be a detective and discover who or what is guilty of killing this tree. You start your investigation by taking a ladder and examining the tree all over carefully. You find evidence of aphids or plant lice eating the leaves of your tree, which is a black walnut, but you do not think there is enough evidence that the aphids are causing the tree to die. Then you find tiny holes or punctures on the small branches, and, by luck, you catch a buffalo tree hopper making these punctures and laying eggs in them.

You see where branches with these punctures in them have died, and you think: "Aha! An open-and-shut case. The buffalo tree hopper is the murderer of this tree!"

Next you find a spray that will kill buffalo tree hoppers and also aphids and other harmful insects, and you carefully spray this tree at regular intervals to get rid of the pests. But the tree continues to die! You have made a mistake, then. You have not found the real murderer. Again you examine the tree carefully all over, but this time you find that many branches have died which are not punctured by the egg-laying of buffalo tree hoppers. Nor can you find any sign of any other creatures attacking these branches, no matter how hard you look. Now it looks like a hopeless case. The tree is dying, but you see no murderer. What can you do?

You can start imagining other ways the tree might be caused to die. Suddenly you think of the roots. You carefully dig down into the ground around some of the roots and you find some of them swollen into knots or galls. Breaking up these swellings you find nothing at first, but under the microscope you see that the roots are infested with tiny worms. These are the worms of the root-knot nematode, whose feeding on the roots of the black walnut are gradually killing the tree. At last you have the real murderer!

But suppose you had not found any root galls. What then? There are at least two other things you could imagine as killers of this tree. One is smog. Sometimes the ingredients in smog, especially where heavily concentrated, actually kill trees. The other possibility might be simply lack of water. The tree might be dying because it had not been watered enough.

Another way to explore in your city can be found in a vacant lot, or a strip of abandoned lawn where a house or building is vacant. In such a place a jungle of weeds has probably grown up. In this jungle there is a constant struggle for survival, not only between the weeds themselves, but between the animals that live there. The series of secret worlds it presents offers fascinating chances for using your detective ability.

Suppose that in a vacant lot you find three piles of debris and in each pile lives a pair of fence lizards. (*Sceloporus.*) You notice that all these fence lizards have some blue on the undersides of their bodies, but the males have much more, their throats in particular being strongly blue. So you ask: "What effect does this blue color have in the lives of these animals?"

You notice that when the sun is shining brightly, one of the lizards often stands on top of a rock or board moving its body up and down and flashing the blue of its throat and belly in the sunlight. So you think maybe this is to frighten away enemies. But careful watching shows that several times a shrike, a large black and white bird, swoops down to try to catch a lizard when it is flashing its blue belly. The flashing of the blue color does not protect the lizard from this bird but actually attracts it.

Soon a small boy runs up and tells you: "Don't touch that lizard. It has a blue belly and that means it is poisonous!" Or course, you know he is wrong, if you have done any studying of lizards, but you think, "Maybe the blue color does do some good by making dogs and cats and similar animals leave the lizard alone because they think it is poisonous." You watch carefully over a period of several days and see both dogs and cats try to catch the lizards even when they are flashing their blue bellies and throats in the sun. So you decide that the blue color has little or no value as protection from enemies.

Using your imagination to find another explanation of the blue color, you think maybe it is useful in some way in signaling to other lizards. By careful watching you soon see that, whenever a lizard is exposing its blue color to flash in the sunlight, there is usually at least one other lizard watching. But what is that flashing of the blue color saying to these other lizards?

You have to lie still for many hours and watch carefully before you find the answer. Finally you see that this flashing of the blue color is done almost entirely by a male, either to attract a female or to threaten other males and try to scare them away from this one male's territory. The female either shows her interest by acting coy and gradually approaching the signaling male, or she shows lack of interest by moving away from him. On the other hand, a nearby male also rises on his legs and begins to flash his blue color as a challenge. If the two males get too close together, they may fight, the winner finally chasing the invading male out of his territory.

You have been a detective. By using your intelligence and imagination and by watching for every detail connected with the dark lives of these lizards, you have finally solved a mystery in a secret world. There are many other such mysteries in the jungle of a vacant lot or abandoned lawn — many of them not yet solved. Why don't you see how good a Sherlock Holmes you can be?

These could be projects among city streets and buildings:

(1) Termites in a section of your city — where they strike and how and what can be done to stop them.

(2) The journeys and hiding places of cockroaches.

(3) The attacks on books by insects in a library and what can be done to prevent them.

(4) The language of city dogs.

(5) Difficulties that plants must overcome when growing in a city, and how they overcome them.

(6) The life of animals, wild and tame, found in one city block (with a map showing where the different kinds live).

IN THE PARKS

Parks in great cities are truly wonderful bits of wildness surrounded by great masses of brick and stone. For example, Golden Gate Park in San Francisco has much secret wildlife, including foxes, raccoons, weasels and other creatures usually found only outside cities.

If you are going to explore your park for secret worlds, one of the first things you should do is to map it, or at least part of it. Make the map of fairly large scale so you can even show individual trees. Any Boy or Girl Scout handbook will tell you how to make a map. Various habitats found in the park should be mapped — such as brushland, coniferous forest, broad-leaved forest, grassland, marsh, ponds, streams, rocky areas, and so forth. Begin to investigate what kinds of animals and plants are found in each of these habitats and what the relationships are between them. Suddenly you will find yourself entering a whole network of secret worlds, any one of which might open a new realm of knowledge.

I remember one afternoon I spent as a boy following a gray squirrel in a park. I moved slowly along with the animal I was watching, stopping when it stopped, and moving when it moved, until finally the squirrel came to think of me as part of the landscape. I discovered that day that my squirrel had a mate who had a nest in a hole in a tree and that she was guarding there some newborn babies. He brought food for her, but sometimes, just like a man, he got so interested in other happenings in the park that he forgot her for a while. Then what an angry chattering she turned on him when he arrived very late and downcast, with his offering of food!

That gray squirrel had a definite territory in the park

Fig. 13. Gray Squirrel.

over which he ruled like a king. He had his nose in every affair in the woods, from a passing rabbit or snake to a group of laughing children, and often told one and all in no uncertain terms that he didn't like this or that about what they did. I don't think anybody satisfied him except me, and that was because he had decided I was just part of the landscape!

Now, unfortunately, I was not at that time a trained explorer, as you are or soon will be, so I didn't ask or try to answer some of these questions about that squirrel: (1) How did he know when danger was coming and what did he do about it? (2) How did he train his children when they grew older, to find food and watch out for danger? (3) How much of this training did he do, himself, and how much and what kind did his mate do? (4) Did he store food for the winter, and, if so, how much of it did he actually use later? (5) How helpful was his carrying around of nuts and seeds in spreading of plants? (6) What were the squirrel's favorite pathways through the trees and why? (7) What was the border of the squirrel's territory and how did he mark the boundaries and keep out enemy squirrels?

A map like the one shown in Figure 14 would answer many of these questions.

Another way your map is useful is for notes on animal coöperation. You will find two kinds of coöperation among the animals you study in a city park: conscious, as when a jay gives warning to other birds of the approach of a cat; and unconscious, as when a large animal, such as a dog, digs up the ground to find food, and un-

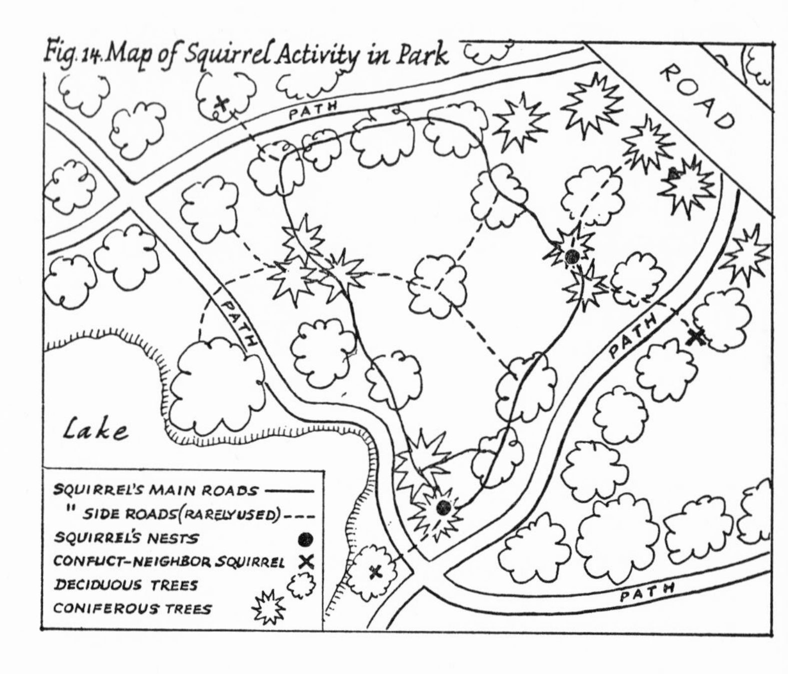

Fig. 14. Map of Squirrel Activity in Park

covers different food for smaller creatures, such as birds to eat.

How do animals help each other in your own city park? You will find out about this by going out into all parts of the park and carefully observing all examples of such cooperation you can find. On the map you have made of the park put a new number every time you find animals coöperating. Ladybird beetles help man by destroying aphids. Woodpeckers help by killing bark-beetle grubs. In your notebook mark down, opposite the number, a full description of the kind of coöperation which you saw. Some will be hidden, and this is where your deductive or Sherlock Holmes power comes into play, for you will have to tell *from little signs* how coöperation is happening. For example, ground squirrels dig holes in the ground, but other animals often use these holes for hiding places too. This is unconscious coöperation. Much of the evidence of it may be found by carefully studying the entranceways of many ground-squirrel holes. At such places you may find not only tracks, but also droppings (each made up of characteristic food remains) of such creatures as white-footed mice, harvest mice, pocket mice, burrowing owls, and others that like to hide or live underground.

As you study further and watch more carefully this matter of animal coöperation, you are likely to find many strange things, some of which may be of great value to science, and some of which may be of benefit to the people who take care of the park. For example, you may find that certain termites are unconsciously helped by other small creatures that kill trees or bushes. When the wood becomes dead, then the termites are able to bore into it and feed upon it. If you could find ways to stop these trees from dying, you could prevent the spread of harmful termites, which often destroy whole buildings. You may find that one kind of bird, such as a woodpecker, furnishes an animal, such as a flying squirrel, a place to live in safety from man and other enemies, so that the flying squirrel would disappear from the park if woodpeckers also disappeared.

Another park project could be a careful study of bird song activity in the spring.

Animals also coöperate with man, usually uncon-

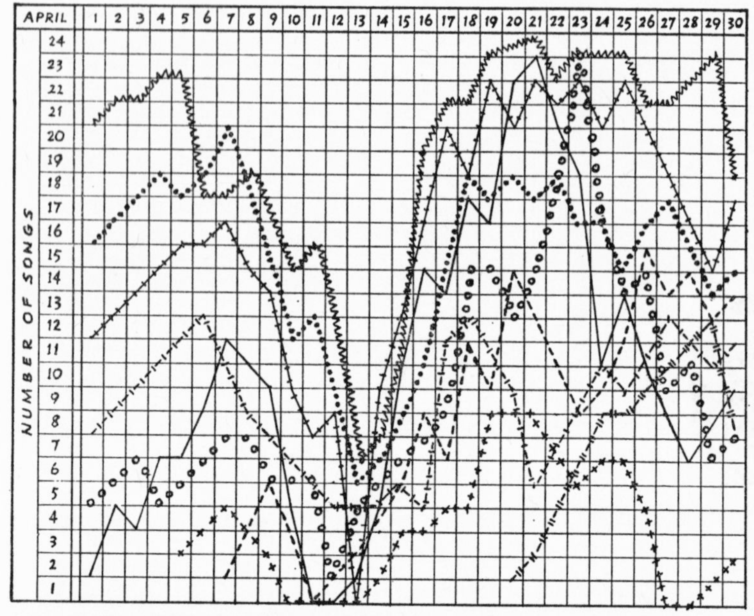

BIRDS OBSERVED AND LISTENED TO EACH MORNING FROM 6 A.M. TO 7 A.M., APRIL 1 TO 15; 5:30 A.M. TO 6:30 A.M., APRIL 16 TO 30: WARBLING VIREO —— PLAIN TITMOUSE ++++ WILSON'S WARBLER--- ORANGE-CROWNED WARBLER.... WESTERN MEADOWLARK oooo RUFOUS-SIDED TOWHEE+++ WREN-TIT ~~~ BROWN TOWHEE -I-I- WH.-CR. SPARROW -II-II-

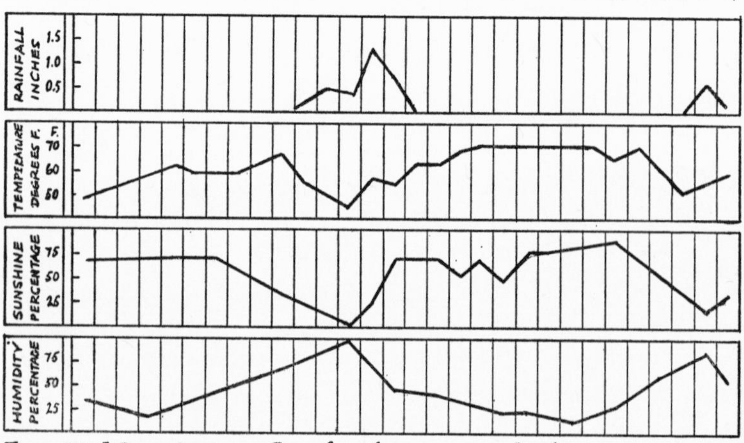

Fig. 15. Bird Song Activity Graph (only most active birds). HABITAT: EDGE OF BRUSHLAND AND GRASSLAND. ACTIVITY OBSERVED DURING APRIL 1961.

sciously. For example, the earthworms in your park are of tremendous value in loosening the soil so as to make it easier for plants to grow. Try to find as many other animals as you can that also coöperate with man, and try to help this coöperation. You can combine a map and a graph, to show where you noticed such coöperation and give information of value about the amount.

Sometimes man's own coöperation with these coöperating animals pays off handsomely. For instance, in some city parks it is the rule to clean thoroughly under all the trees and bushes, leaving no debris anywhere, but certain kinds of debris may provide good hiding places for animals that are coöperative, such as insect-eating birds and mammals that help keep the park rid, for the most part, of pests. It also often forms hiding places for animals that are interesting to watch, such as shrews, and so adds to the entertainment and educational value of the park. Your exploration and understanding of this secret world may give you the information needed to convince park officials that they should make certain changes in park rules that will be to the benefit of all by making a more interesting park.

Finally, as a result of your careful researches, you should be able to put together all the information about animal coöperation in the park which you have gathered. This might include showing the laws under which such coöperation worked, or making charts and graphs that showed how efficient such coöperation was and how useful to both the animals and to man.

(WARNING: In certain areas of our country bats, skunks and other small mammals occasionally catch the disease

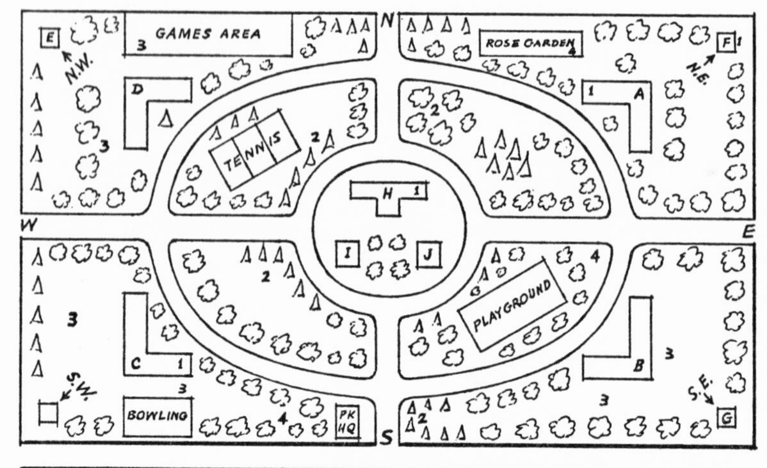

ITEM	STATUS OF BATTLE				
	MAY 1, 1961	MAY 15, 1961	JUNE 1, 1961	JUNE 15, 1961	JUL. 1, 1961
1. TERMITES	DAMAGE TO BLDGS A AND C	DAMAGE STOPPED IN A AND C	DAMAGE SEEN IN BLDG F	DAMAGE VERY BAD IN BLDG F	CONTROL STARTED
2. BARK BEETLES	INFESTATION BAD IN TREES N.E. OF H.	INFESTATION WORSE, SPREADS TO TREES N.W. AND W.	WOODPECKERS HELPING ATTACKS. TREES SPRAYED TO STOP INFEST'N.	IMPROVEMENT IN NW, NE, BUT NEW INFESTATION IN CONIFERS TO S.	
3. GOPHERS	HOLES BAD AT ALL PLACES NUMBERED	GOPHERS TRAP'D OUT AT NW, BUT STILL BAD IN SE	HOLES STILL BAD IN SE BECAUSE OF CLEVER GOPHER	LAST BAD GO-PHER TRAPPED IN S.E.	NEW GOPHER IN S.W.
4. APHIDS	VERY BAD IN-FESTATION IN ROSE GARDEN	ROSE GARDEN SPRAYED. IN-FESTATION DIS-COVERED IN S.	ROSE GARDEN STILL INFESTED. LADYBIRD BEE-TLES INTRODUCED	INFESTATION STARTS IN E. ROSE GARDEN ALMOST CLEAR.	MORE LADYBIRD BEETLES INTROD.

Fig. 16. War Map—Park Gardeners vs. Animals, DECIDUOUS TREE ✿ CONIFER Δ
ILLUSTRATING CO-OPERATION OF ANIMALS WITH MAN.

of rabies, and a bite from one of these animals can be very dangerous unless proper precautions are taken. If you are bitten, immediately notify the nearest doctor and have him look after you. The animal should be killed and its head given to the County Health Service for examination. Tularemia and Rocky Mountain Spotted Fever (from ticks) are other diseases that come from small mammals, particularly rodents and rabbits. Ask your County Health Service for information about these diseases in your county and avoid capturing or touching any animals that might be carrying these diseases. Many interesting explorations of wild animal life can be done entirely by observation, without ever having to touch the animals involved.)

4

SECRET WORLDS OF THE COUNTRYSIDE

If you live in the country or visit a ranch or farm or national park or forest for a long time in the summer, your opportunities for exploring secret worlds become tremendous in number. I remember my first real summer in the country, when I was nine. It was on a huge cattle ranch in the middle of the southern Nevada sagebrush region, a place with a hot-water creek running through it and towering mountains on all sides. It was a wonderful place for a boy. Shoshone Indians were living there still in their ancient stick-and-mud-huts. Wild horses, or mustangs as they were called, raced through the sagebrush, and there were many ranch horses that a half-breed boy of my age and I used to ride.

I remember the deep, rich smell of fresh-cut alfalfa hay, and I remember chasing a baby rabbit in and out among the cut stalks; I remember the wild howling of coyotes on a distant butte when the moon was round and golden over Shoshone Mountain, and the long trek we made with the cowboys and a jangling, clanging chuck wagon up to Wild Horse Creek where trout leaped crazily from white waters and came to us later delicious from the frying pan.

In such a place I was surrounded by thousands of secret worlds waiting to be explored, but I was so wound up in the newness and wildness of living on a great cattle ranch that I knew little about them. Now I can look back and see some of the things I missed. There was the mysterious hot creek itself, welling up out of the ground at the base of Shoshone Mountain and winding down through the ranch from deep pool to deep pool, giving out always a faint smell of sulphur. Cattails grew along its rim and other water plants, and in its blue depths blue-green algae formed ghostlike, waving clusters. What creatures lived in those hot waters and what did they live on and how did they become accustomed to the heat?

Out in the sagebrush, stretching up to the pinyon pines and junipers of the middle slopes of Shoshone Mountain, life lay quiet and mostly invisible during the heat of the summer day. But at eveningtime, when the long shadows fell over the sweet-smelling sage, kangaroo

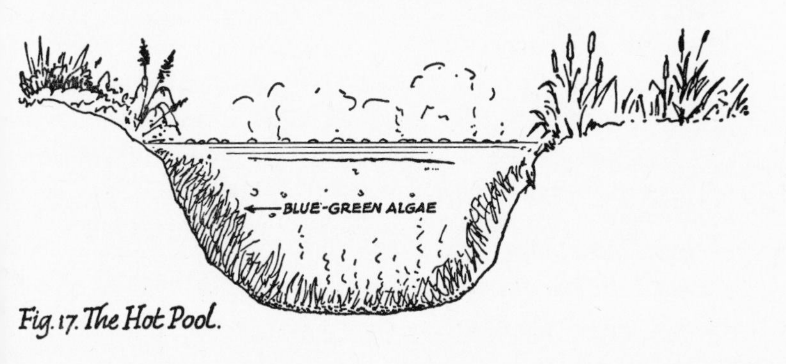

Fig. 17. The Hot Pool.

rats crept out of their hidden burrows and danced in the moonlight, big-eared kit foxes drifted through the brush like gray smoke to pounce on the rats, and Old Man Coyote trotted along trying to sniff out sleeping Jack rabbits. Strange snakes of the night left their winding trails in the dust, seeking for pocket mice and giant insects. And every one of them lived in a secret world to be explored.

What other explorations could you make inspired by adventures in the countryside?

Twice I have been followed by mountain lions, once in the San Jacinto Mountains in southern California where we found the big round tracks of the lion on top of our own footprints in the snow. The other time was in the Yolla Bolly Mountains of northwestern California, where a mountain lion followed me for three hours when I walked alone over the mountain in the moonlight. At the top of the pass the hair along my neck shivered when I saw the huge, ugly head of the lion cast a black shadow square across the face of the full moon! Do you know how many records there are of lions following men? And what variations, due to difference of character in the lions have appeared in the different records? This kind of exploration could be done mainly by correspondence and by careful research in magazines and books that deal with wildlife.

One day in the great plains of eastern Colorado I spent an afternoon watching the gyrating dances of

Fig. 18. "... I Saw the Huge, Ugly Head of the Lion...."

white-throated swifts as they hunted for insects high in the clear blue sky. Swerving, twisting, swirling, turning, darting down like meteors, and then up like rockets, they formed so beautiful and graceful a pattern of flight that I stood spellbound for hours. Down from the

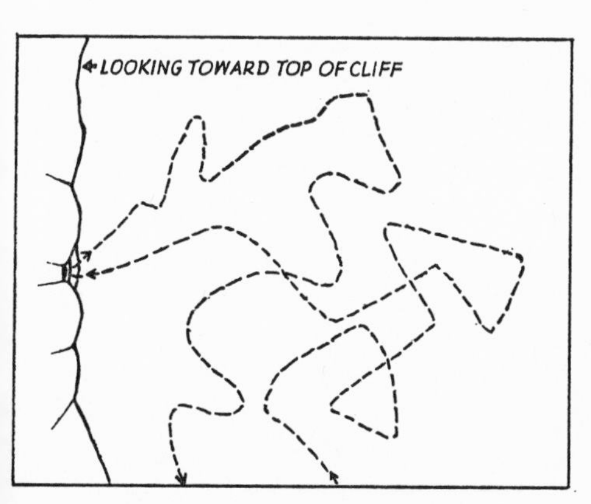

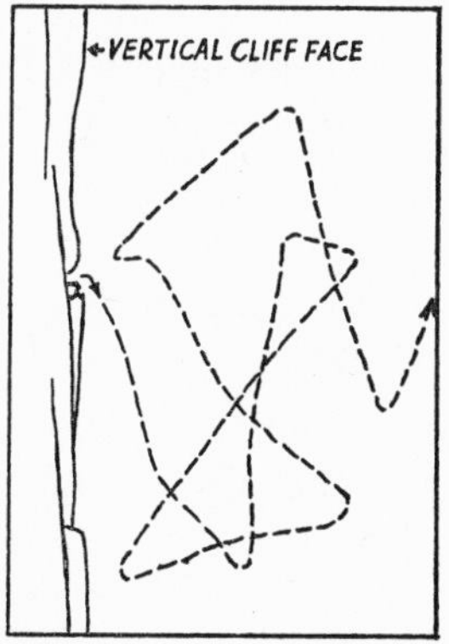

Fig. 19. Flight Pattern of Swifts – LEFT: FROM BELOW – RIGHT: FROM SIDE.

heights came their high twittering calls, changing and varying to suit their emotions. I knew that these birds were true aeronauts, spending all their lives high in the air, either in the sky itself or nesting hundreds of feet up on great cliffs. Not once did I see a swift alight on a treetop or rock or give any indication of doing so. Surely these creatures are only slightly of this earth!

Some of the questions that might be asked about swifts are: (1) How do they signal to each other — and what are these signals for? (2) Is there any organized plan about their method of flying — or do they form those great groups high in the sky just for company? (3) Over what kind of country and in what kind of weather do they usually hunt for food — and just what do they like to feed on? (4) How do they build and maintain their nests? All of these questions would probably need a good pair of field glasses and probably also a telescope to be answered adequately.

In California there are great hairy spiders called tarantulas, often three or four inches in leg spread, that wander slowly about during the warm part of the year. Most people are deathly afraid of these creatures, but they are really rather harmless. Even the bite of one is not as bad as a bee's sting, and they will not bite unless teased to do so. I have many times let them walk perfectly harmlessly over my hands and arms.

One day I followed one of these great spiders for several hours. The results of this following are shown on my map of the journey. (See Figure 20.) The spider was hunting for whatever large insects he could find in

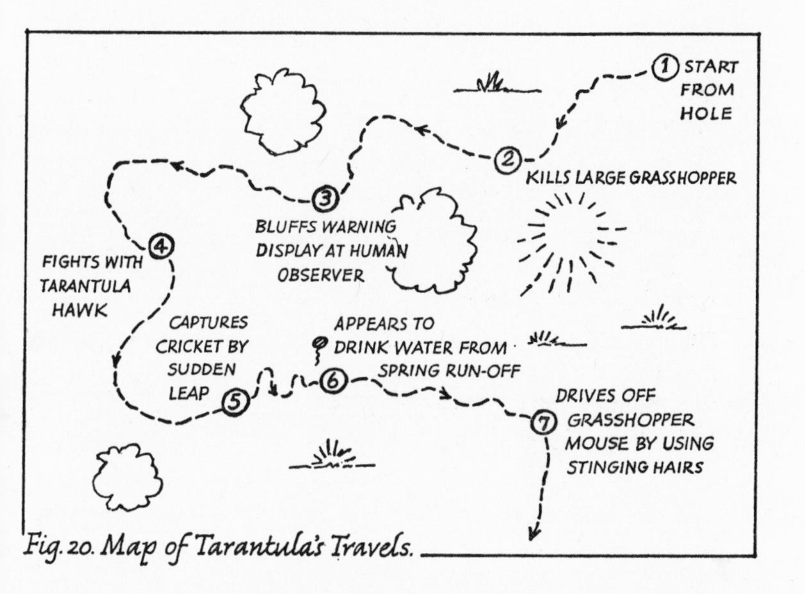

Fig. 20. Map of Tarantula's Travels.

the dried grass of the hillside. For the most part he moved about quite slowly, feeling ahead of him with long legs and appearing to test the air with his feelers. But when a grasshopper moved nearby he would suddenly jump forward. Usually the grasshopper would escape by the jump it made, but twice I saw hoppers become entangled in the grass in their hurry to escape and then the tarantula rushed forward and seized them quickly. He would sink his long black fangs into his victim and the poison soon ended its struggles. He would then masticate around the wound with his mandibles and apparently put some kind of digestive fluid inside the body of the grasshopper, which would allow him to suck out the juices of the body.

In a place where a spring of water had produced some green grass the tarantula met a field mouse face to face as the mouse was running along one of its grassy tunnels. When the mouse's nose touched the leg of the giant spider, the spider spun about swiftly and struck at the mouse with its jaws. The mouse jumped back with a squeak of fear, but I noticed that some of the hair of the spider had brushed off on the mouse's nose. The last sight I had of the mouse it was vigorously trying to rub the hairs off its face, acting as if they were as irritating as nettles. I knew that there was an irritating poison in the hairs of the tarantula and that it used these hairs to defend itself against enemies, particularly small mammals.

This long-legged male spider I was watching was attacked near evening by a great black-and-orange wasp called a tarantula hawk. The wasp hovered over the spider for a minute, then landed deliberately in front of him and advanced to the attack. The spider rose as high as he could on his legs, lifted the front legs toward the

Fig. 21. Tarantula vs. Tarantula Hawk.

wasp and waved them, at the same time showing his long, curved black fangs. The wasp tried to rush forward and grab the spider in such a way that she could throw her abdomen with the sting on the tip under the spider's body and sting it in the abdomen, but the spider pushed her away with his long legs and tried to bite her. The wasp bit the spider in one leg and held off the fierce jaws with her own legs, but she could not bring her sting near enough to get in a fatal blow.

Over and over on the ground the two rolled, first one on top and then the other, each holding its enemy far enough away to keep from getting seriously hurt. The wasp broke away and came again at the spider from another angle, and again there was the fierce struggle of waving legs, darting sting and clashing fangs. I expected at any instant to see one or the other killed or paralyzed, but somehow they avoided each other's lethal weapons. At last the wasp broke free from the tarantula, gave up and flew away. The spider wandered off and disappeared under some thick brush.

The result of the battle was quite amazing. Usually one of these fierce wasps will paralyze the spider it attacks by putting the sting into a large nerve ganglion on the underside of the abdomen.

Watching a tarantula for one afternoon was, of course, only the beginning of exploration into this secret world. Many questions needed to be asked and answered, such as: (1) Was the spider also seeking a mate as well as hunting? (2) What is the chief insect food of the spider and does it help mankind by the creatures it kills? (3) Does the spider have different means of defense for different enemies, and what are they and how successful are they? (The chart shown in Figure 22 shows two means of defense used by the tarantula against enemies, and shows the results of a study made to determine how often this defense was successful and why.) This is just one adventure suggesting one way to explore a countryside secret world and record your findings.

There are others. For instance, one evening I sat in an isolated cabin in the wilderness of the Santa Cruz Mountains in California watching a big yellow tomcat stretched lazily on the sill of an open window. Suddenly, without the slightest warning, a huge wildcat showed its snarling whiskered face at the window, seized the startled tom in claws and jaws, crushed its back with one crunching bite that stilled a startled squall. The wildcat rushed off into the woods with its prey. Both the horror of this sight and a question regarding it have recurred to me often since then. What effect do wildcats have on the population of tame cats in the country? It would take a lot of correspondence and research over a wide area as well as some personal observation and research to find even a

ACTION OF TARANTULA IN SELF-DEFENSE	SEPARATE OBSERVATIONS
1. T. HIDES IN HOLE WHILE T. HAWK STALKS OUTSIDE (UNSUCCESSFUL: T. WAS MADE TO COME OUT AND FIGHT)	● ● ● × ● ×
2. T. DRIVES OFF SMALL MOUSE WITH ITS STINGING HAIRS (UNSUCCESSFUL: T. RETREATED FROM MOUSE)	● × ● ●
3. T. FRIGHTENS OFF HUMAN (NOT OBSERVER) BY BRISTLING, LIFTING LEGS, EXPOSING SHARP JAWS	× ● ● ● ×
4. T. FENDS OFF T. HAWK WITH ITS LONG LEGS WHILE LYING ON BACK, FANGS EXPOSED FOR BITING	● ● × (T. KILLED BY T. HAWK)

Fig. 22. Chart of Tarantula's Defenses. SUCCESSFUL ● UNSUCCESSFUL ×

partial answer to this question, but it would be another fascinating world to explore.

The rustle of tiny feet in the long grass and the padding of larger feet in the forest, the song of the mockingbird in the moonlight and the mysterious "Pu-wooo!" of the whippoorwill in the dawn are likewise calls to adventure and exploration. Here are only a few suggestions of specific explorations you might make:

(1) Study the trails of certain animals — how they make them and why they use them.

(2) Study the rocks of a given square mile area —

Fig. 23. The Wildcat Rushed off into the Woods with its Prey.

try to determine where they came from and how they got there.

(3) Study the camouflage of insects in your neighborhood — how it helps them escape enemies or capture prey.

(4) Explore colors in nature — how they are used by animals and plants to attract, to repel or to hide.

(5) Find the stories told by animal tracks in the mud along a creek bank or in the snow.

(6) Find the most successful plants in your area and determine why they are so successful.

(7) Study and map the life of an acre of ground thoroughly.

One field of exploration which has been only partly touched is that of bird habits and flight. There are many species about whom little or nothing is known. Great patience is required to follow one kind of bird for days and days, watching everything it does, keeping careful notes such as those in Figure 24. Blinds need to be built to watch the bird's nesting habits (See Figure 25) and other activities. There are many remarkable individuals among birds — the wise old crow, the saucy and excitable chickadee, the secretive vireo, the fierce and implacable goshawk. Significant movements to watch among birds are the signal of flashing feathers, the comical flutterings and cryings of a mother and father bird to lure their youngsters into making their first flights, the spiraling, whistling dives and gyrations of mating hawks, the endless food-hunting activities of nuthatches, the expressions in the eyes of wrens that tell you about

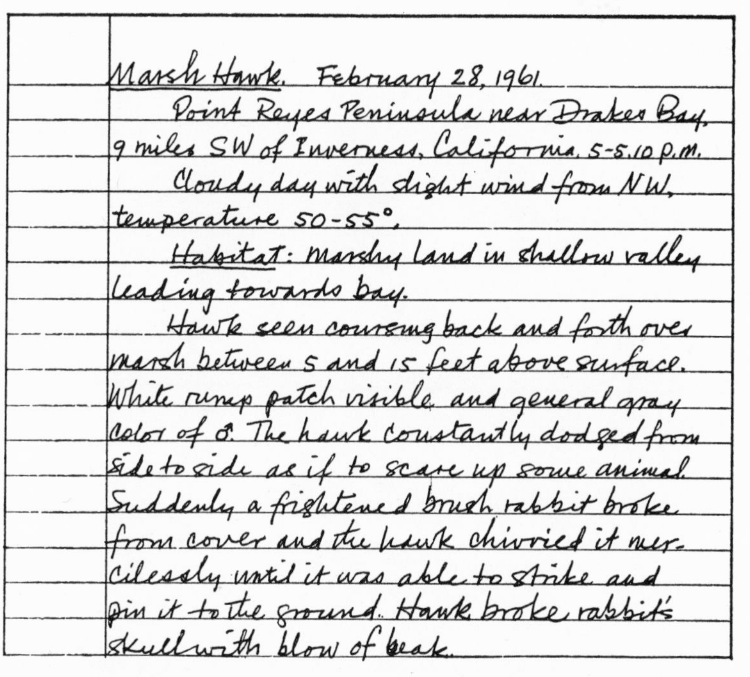
Marsh Hawk. February 28, 1961.
Point Reyes Peninsula near Drakes Bay,
9 miles SW of Inverness, California. 5-5.10 p.m.
Cloudy day with slight wind from NW,
temperature 50-55°.
Habitat: Marshy land in shallow valley
leading towards bay.
Hawk seen coursing back and forth over
marsh between 5 and 15 feet above surface.
White rump patch visible and general gray
color of ♂. The hawk constantly dodged from
side to side as if to scare up some animal.
Suddenly a frightened brush rabbit broke
from cover and the hawk chivvied it mer-
cilessly until it was able to strike and
pin it to the ground. Hawk broke rabbit's
skull with blow of beak.

Fig. 24, Bird Notes. SAMPLE PAGE OF A NATURALIST'S FIELD NOTE BOOK.

their emotions, as do also the flicking movements of their tails and wings. Each individual bird also has individual characteristics that help to separate it from others of its own kind, just as your actions and mannerisms distinguish you from other human beings. Very careful watching is needed to tell these differences, but rich will be your rewards in new knowledge.

Suppose you discovered the nest of a pair of sparrow hawks and watched them for several weeks in the spring-

Fig 25. Blinds for Bird Observation and Photography.

THESE MAY BE IMPROVISED, AND VARIED, ACCORDING TO THE SITUATION AND MATERIALS AT HAND. THEY SHOULD BE INCONSPICUOUS AND CONCEAL THE OBSERVER'S MOVEMENTS.

time. Your day-by-day notes of their habits and activities might come out in the form of graphs and maps such as those shown in Figure 26. Note how each graph and map helps give you an intimate picture of the life of these birds during the period in which you have watched them, including related facts of weather and human interference.

Mendel, the famous Austrian botanist, discovered in the 1870's the tremendous secret of how plant and animal inheritance is passed on from one plant or animal to another. He showed, for example, what kinds of hy-

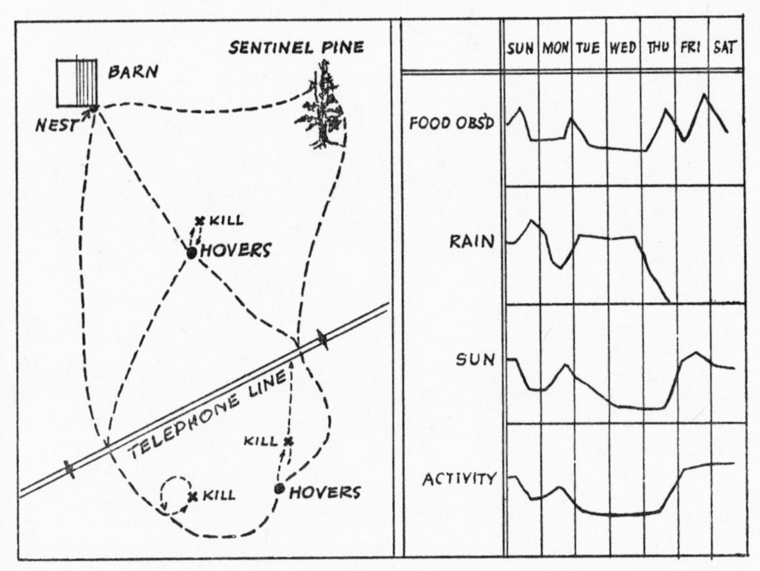

Fig. 26 Map of Territory and Graph of Activity of Sparrow Hawk.

brids were produced when white-flowered peas were crossed with red-flowered peas, and what would happen in future generations. He developed what are today called Mendel's Laws of Inheritance. (Figure 27.) Unfortunately, even scientists are sometimes blind to new discoveries of great significance, and nobody paid any attention to Mendel's findings until many years after his death When Mendel's laws were rediscovered in the twentieth century it was found that they could be used to develop all kinds of new plants and animals of great benefit to man. The famous botanist, Burbank, used them to develop giant strawberries and tomatoes, especially fine

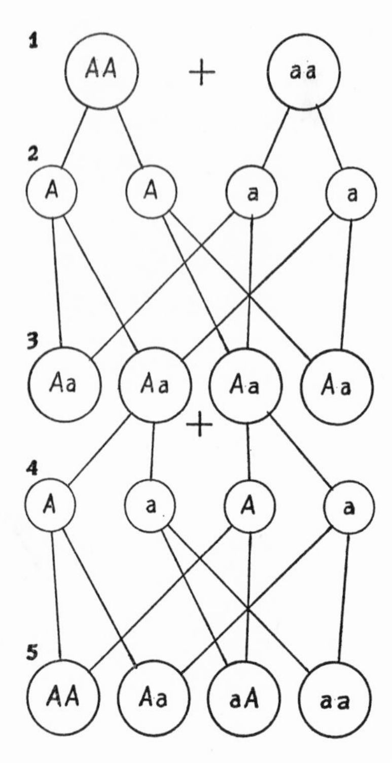

Fig. 27. Mendel's Laws of Inheritance: DIAGRAM OF EXPERIMENT SHOWING TRANSMISSION OF DOMINANT (A) AND RECESSIVE (a) CHARACTERS.

1. PURE-BRED TALL (AA) AND SHORT (aa) PEAS GIVING, 2, SEX CELLS A AND a RESPECTIVELY, ARE MATED, THEIR OFFSPRING, 3, ARE ALL TALL BECAUSE TALLNESS IS DOMINANT, BUT THEIR GENES CONTAIN THE RECESSIVE (a) FACTOR TO PRODUCE, 4, SEX CELLS a AS WELL AS A.

WHEN A PAIR OF THESE IS MATED, THEIR OFFSPRING, 5, WILL COME TALL AND SHORT IN THE RATIO OF 3 TO 1. (OTHER CHARACTERS ARE RED VS. WHITE, SMOOTH VS. WRINKLED PEAS, ETC.)

(MODIFIED FROM *THE DOUBLEDAY PICTORIAL LIBRARY OF NATURE: EARTH, PLANTS, ANIMALS*, 1961)

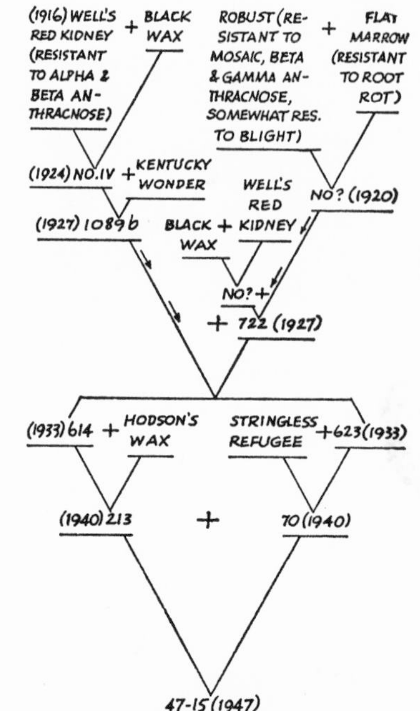

Fig. 28. Development of a New Type of Plant (Snap Bean No. 47-15) by Selective Breeding.

CHART SHOWS THE ANCESTRY OF AN IMPROVED STRAIN OR TYPE OF BEAN DEVELOPED THROUGH 21 YEARS OF EFFORT BY R. A. EMERSON. (AFTER H. M. MUNGER, AS REPRODUCED IN SRB AND OWEN: *GENERAL GENETICS*, W. H. FREEMAN AND COMPANY, SAN FRANCISCO, 1952)

ears of corn, and so on, giving better food to the world.

Similar work is now being done with animals and plants of many kinds, but only a small beginning has yet been made. Wonderful discoveries are waiting for the explorer who can learn to breed and develop new kinds of plants and animals. For example, the search is on all over the world by entomologists to develop new varieties of insects that will help kill other insects that are harmful to man. For your own experiments, insects have the advantage of producing several generations in a year, so that breeding experiments can be done in a shorter time than with most other animals.

The accompanying diagram (Figure 28) shows how one scientist developed a new kind of bean by breeding together the types that carried the inheritance he wanted to develop. It is impossible in a small book to show in detail how such complicated experiments can be carried out, but there are books that specialize in such knowledge and to these you may wish to turn (see list at the end of this book).

One of the least-explored secret worlds of the countryside is the world of the night. As a matter of fact, most mammals of your neighborhood come out only at night, and there are great numbers of insects, birds, reptiles, amphibians and other creatures that do the same.

Coming home to my cabin in the jungles of Panama by night I was at first unnerved by the strange feeling of the dark jungle, the queer little noises in the forest, the startled and loud squawk of a paca leaping out from under my feet, the green and red lights of flying click beetles, the mysterious shadows, and particularly the long, snakelike vines hanging down from the jungle tops. One night the Guaymia Indian boy who was working for me ran ahead of me and reached the cabin some minutes before I did. When I was about a hundred yards from the cabin, what seemed to be an immense snake fell out of the darkness upon my shoulders. With a scream of fear, I fought it off, and beat all records getting to the cabin! There I found Chio rolling on the ground, roaring with laughter. He had set a trap for me, and caused a big jungle vine to drop out of a tree onto my shoulders!

After that, somehow, my fear of the jungle dark began to go away. I had been using a flashlight to find my way along the trail, but I found that, without light, my eyes became surprisingly accustomed to the darkness. Moving through the forest without a light, I was able to surprise or see many animals that would have otherwise fled from me. I discovered that I could now sense the presence of animals which with the light my senses had failed to notice. By standing perfectly still, for example, I was able once to watch a large mother tapir, an animal as big as a cow, and her young one slip down through the trees to the jungle river and swim across in the moonlight.

The chief animal to fear by night in the forests, fields or deserts of North America is the rattlesnake. But there is little danger to the person who moves through the darkness slowly and cautiously. Every rattlesnake has a built-in warning system, a pit in the nose that detects from many feet away the heat of another body. If the intruder is large, the rattlesnake quickly moves out of its way, or if it comes too close, the snake sounds a warning with rattles. Of course, if you hear a slithering sound among the leaves you should turn on your flashlight and see if the sound is made by a dangerous snake.

My wife was trapped one night on top of a high butte in the great plains of eastern Colorado by literally hundreds of rattlesnakes who had come to the butte, that fall, to den up in its rocky crevices. She had gone to the butte to watch for some lost horses and was without any light. On all sides she heard the sibilant sounds of the great snakes. If she had given way to fear, she might have run screaming into the midst of them or lost her mind. Fortunately she understood snakes and knew, first, that they move comparatively slowly; second, that they do not attack unless they think you are about to attack them; and third, that they almost always warn you before they strike.

With this knowledge, it was not too difficult for her to escape from the butte. Moving very slowly and cautiously, she picked up small pebbles and threw them about her in the darkness. Where the pebbles did not arouse rattles from rattlesnakes, she moved forward. The places where rattling sounded she avoided. Thus, down the butte she went in the darkness and to safety. Remember this story when you are out at night and hear a rattlesnake near you. There is very little danger if you act with courage, caution and intelligence.

Another way to see in the darkness without being seen is to use a red flashlight. The red light does not bother most animals, many of whom cannot even see it, but it gives enough light for a man to watch them. To keep from being smelled by wild animals, rub your body and clothing with a strong-smelling plant such as sagebrush. If your clothes are soaked in water in which such a plant has been boiled, this will kill the man smell even more effectively.

Little is known about many animals that come out at night. Among the life histories about which least is known are those of the night snakes. We do know that these creatures have eyes like cats with irises that can be opened very widely to let in the light. They crawl quietly through the darkness looking for large night insects, salamanders, and small mammals. Much careful night exploration will be needed to find out more about their habits and reactions.

Bats are also fascinating, little-known creatures to watch by night. A good pair of field glasses are useful in the early evening. Soon you will begin to find out that different bats fly at different times of the night and have quite different habits. In one habitat the tiny pipistrels (light-colored) come out at the first hint of dusk and fly very erratically, darting and dodging about catching insects. In another habitat the little brown bats appear first, not so erratic, but still flying in zigzags. Then come the big brown bats and the pallid bats, the big browns flying with straight, almost clumsy flight, while the large, light-colored pallid bats fly almost as erratically as the tiny, yellow pipistrels. The pallid bats like to fly along the edges of the hills, while the pipistrels always come down into the center of a valley, seeking especially for swamps or marshes where the insects are thick. Most bats like to

Fig. 29. Common American Bats

THE PIPISTREL MAY APPEAR WITH THE SUN'S LAST RAYS, FOLLOWED BY THE LITTLE BROWN, THE BIG BROWN, THE PALLID, AND FINALLY THE HOARY BAT. (SILHOUETTES ADAPTED FROM COLLINS: *FIELD GUIDE TO AMERICAN WILDLIFE.*)

live in caves, but some, like the red bats and hoary bats, hang and hide in trees.

The habits, living places and other interesting details of the lives of bats in your neighborhood can be explored by you as another secret world. Some of the questions you might want to ask and answer are: (1) What time of night do the different species fly and why? (2) How can you tell the difference between the different species just by watching their flight? (3) What kind of places do the local bats like to sleep or hibernate in? Show this on a map or diagram. (4) What bats like most to feed on mosquitoes, and how effective are they in getting rid of these pests? (4) Which bats hibernate in your area in the winter, and which go south in winter? (5) Can the method of catching food of each type of bat be diagrammed?

5

SECRET WORLDS OF OTHER STATES AND COUNTRIES

IN the great age of the ancient Greeks people were corresponding with each other about science. They even sent specimens of animals and plants and rocks and minerals back and forth by the crude mail of those days, and talked of many things in the universe, from giant planets and suns to tiny, almost invisible insects. In those times the first scientific books were written, but they were written by hand on parchment and rarely were more than two or three copies made. It was thus very difficult for students in different parts of the then known world to keep up on existing knowledge, even though that was only a tiny fraction of the scientific knowledge we have today. The ancient Greeks finally moved all their scientific manuscripts or copies of them to the great library at Alexandria in Egypt. Here for several centuries students could go for scientific study, and here was concentrated most of the knowledge of the world. Unfortunately this marvelous library, filled with books that today would be worth ten times their weight in solid gold, was burned down in the fourth century. And with that burning, science almost vanished from the world.

Today we have thousands of copies of each scientific book, and, in most large libraries, we can find practically the complete knowledge of many generations of scholars and scientists. This is the basis of our world civilization. In these libraries we can learn the life habits of the dingoes of Australia, or about the wonderful emeralds of Colombia and how they were mined by both ancient Chibchan Indians and the modern mestizo of Colombia. Even though we do not actually travel to these countries, we can, by study and research, become experts on many things that are found in them. From your own room, by the aid of both books and faraway friends, you can travel over seas, cross great continents, explore deep jungles and climb marvelous mountains, developing, as you do so, knowledge that may be completely new to the world and sometimes of great value.

To do this correctly and to the fullest extent you must develop the mind of a trained scientist. We have already touched in the first chapter on how the mind of a scientist works, how he is at one and the same time both completely open-minded and cautiously skeptical of his own findings and those of others. We have seen how the scientific method, used by a real scientist, is the application of infinite patience and infinite painstaking exploration on all sides of a subject. But the one quality needed above all others by the scientist, amateur or otherwise, who studies the animals or the plants, rocks or minerals of a distant region, without being able to visit it, is the ability to *synthesize*. To synthesize means, quite simply, to take separate parts of a problem or phenomena and put them together into an intelligent and reasonable whole. This is the opposite of another useful tool of the scientist, *analysis,* or the ability to break the whole down into its parts.

I want to give you an example of synthesis on a rather grand scale so that you will be able to understand it fully. Suppose you wrote to correspondents on isolated islands all over the world, such as Easter Island, Rapa and Chatham Islands in the South Pacific, Cocos Island and the Seychelles Islands in the Indian Ocean, and South Georgia Island and Tristan da Cunha Island in the South Atlantic. Most of the people of these islands talk English, but those on Easter Island speak Spanish so you would need to know how to read Spanish or know somebody living near you who can translate Spanish for you. You would write to people on these islands and ask them to find out for you the answers to certain questions about the animal and plant life there. (NOTE: You can see these islands marked on any good map of the world.)

Here are samples of the questions: What are the most successful animals in your island — and what are their characteristics? What families of animals are found on your island — and what are the differences between members of the same family? What animals live permanently on your island — and what animals spend only part of the year there? What kinds of camouflage do the animals on your island use to protect themselves from enemies? How do the month-to-month changes in climate affect the animal life of your island? What special physical characteristics have animals on the island developed to adapt themselves to that special environment? How many different species of animals in each family are there on your island?

As you received answers to these various questions you would put them in the form of graphs, and these graphs would begin to synthesize your isolated facts into meaningful wholes, as you can see from the illustrations Figure 30. At last you would make the final synthesis of all the facts you have been collecting from isolated islands and come up with something like this:

1. There are only a few species of animals on an isolated island because of the difficulty of animals' reaching the island over the ocean.

ISLAND:	A	B	C	D	E	F	G	TROPICAL MAINLAND
FERTILE AREA—SQUARE MILES	16	2	20	18	28	3	31	3,000,000
MOST SUCCESSFUL BIRD & ANIMAL	FINCH RAT	PENGUIN RAT	PIGEON RAT	FINCH RAT	FINCH RAT	PENGUIN RAT	PARROT RAT	PARROT RAT
NO. OF BIRD AND ANIMAL SPECIES—								
CARNIVORES	1			1	2		2	228
HERBIVORES	4	3	10	6	9	3	11	2,120
INSECTIVORES	1	1	2	1	2		3	743
OMNIVORES	3	1	3	3	3	1	4	1,002
ANIMALS & BIRDS USING CAMOUFLAGE	2	0	0	2	2	0	3	2,850
YEARLY ANIMAL ACTIVITY FROM WINTER TO WINTER								
SPECIES SUCCESSFUL ON ISLANDS BUT NOT ON MAINLAND	8	4	10	12	13	3	16	
RAINFALL								

Fig. 30. Graphs on Isolated Islands, mostly Tropical (THIS IS AN IMAGINARY GRAPH OF IMAGINARY ISLANDS FOR THE SAKE OF ILLUSTRATION).

2. There may be only one family of permanent birds and one or two families of permanent mammals, one family of reptiles and one family of amphibians — showing that probably at one time in the distant past ancestors of each of these families came to each island.

3. Camouflage on isolated islands is practically nonexistent because the animals have so few enemies that few of them need to protect themselves in this way.

4. When only one family of birds or mammals is found on an isolated island, this family often splits up into divisions that parallel much larger divisions on the mainland. For example there are birds of the same family that fill the same functions on the isolated island that are filled on the mainland by hawks, owls, flycatchers, kingfishers, finches. (See Figure 31.)

5. Animals on islands with extremes of temperature and climate protect themselves in much the same way as animals on the mainland; they either hibernate or they migrate when the cold weather comes, but the migrating animals are those found over wide areas of the world, while the hibernating species are found only on the isolated island.

6. Animals on an isolated island often lose characteristics that were originally useful to their kind on the mainland. So some birds become wingless because wings are no longer necessary to escape from enemies, and some reptiles lose warning colorations or defensive frills that were once useful to their ancestors (Figure 32).

With these conclusions built up from a large group of apparently isolated facts, you now have several syntheses or overall pictures of life on isolated islands. You find

Fig. 31. Island Family of Birds (HAWAIIAN SICKLEBILLS) BREAKING UP INTO MAJOR TYPES—THE EVOLUTIONARY PROCESS OF ADAPTIVE RADIATION (AFTER KEULEMANNS IN LACK: *DARWIN'S FINCHES*, CAMBRIDGE, 1947).

that island life is surprisingly similar even though the islands are so separated by immense distances and so surrounded by wide reaches of sea that there can be practically no contact between them. You come to the general conclusion that like conditions in the world produce like results on animal life.

These facts and conclusions have already been reached by scientists, so what I have given here is nothing new; but the exercises we have just gone through in gathering facts are helpful in showing how a similar but never-before-made exploration might develop into a new under-

Fig. 32. New Zealand's Kiwi Has Wings too Small for Flight.

standing of life in the world through a synthesis of numerous small facts.

HOW TO COMMUNICATE WITH PEOPLE IN DISTANT PLACES ABOUT SCIENTIFIC PROBLEMS

English is spoken over most of the earth, but it is very wise for every human being to learn at least one language besides his own so that he may have the joy and pleasure of communicating with people of different culture and outlook. Spanish is my second language. Yours might be French or German or Russian or Japanese, but whatever it is choose one that interests you and whose people you would like to visit and talk with.

Following are ways to find the people with whom you would like to correspond:

(1) Use the *Naturalist's Directory,* published by Jerrold Oakley, Box 418, Armonk, N. Y., and on the

shelves of most libraries, to find the names and addresses of naturalists in distant states or foreign countries. Write a courteous letter explaining what you would like to explore in a certain naturalist's state or country, and offering in exchange to send him specimens or photos of animals, plants, rocks, minerals or fossils from your area. Ask him, if he himself is not interested, to send you the names and addresses of other naturalists in his vicinity who might be able to help you out.

(2) Write to the Chamber of Commerce of a city or town of a distant state or province and ask them to recommend a local naturalist, such as a high school biology teacher, or a local taxidermist, to whom you could write. When you write to this person again ask courteously for coöperation in your exploration, offering to send exchange material or do other services for him, and request the names and addresses of other naturalists in case he is not interested.

(3) Write to the Foreign Office of a foreign government in the capital city of that country and ask for information about naturalists or naturalist organizations in that country, politely requesting their names and addresses. If possible send international exchange stamps, which you can usually obtain at your post office, so you pay for the return postage. Write to the addresses given you and again politely request their coöperation plus the names and addresses of other interested naturalists who might be able to help you.

(4) If you get an inadequate answer from the Foreign Office, you should write next to the Department of Agriculture, since this department often has various

scientists on its staff from whom you may get coöperation.

(5) Ask your librarian for a reference book that lists the names and addresses of universities and colleges in distant states and foreign countries. Write to the Zoology, Botany, Paleontology, Archaeology or Geology Departments of these institutions, depending on where your interests lie, asking them how you may contact individuals who will help you with your exploration. Be sure to be very courteous and tell them that you would be glad to exchange specimens or information about your area or do other services for the information you want. (For exchanging specimens with naturalists in distant places see the instructions given in my *Amateur Naturalist's Handbook.*)

Here are a few explorations you might then undertake:

(1) Make a study of animal adaptation to different ecological conditions in a given area of a foreign country or a different state as compared to a similar area in your neighborhood. To make this very simple you could take just one animal, such as the field or meadow mouse. First study the principal species of these mice found in your area until you become fairly well acquainted with their habits and how they adapt themselves to local habitats and climate. Then write to a naturalist in another state or a foreign country where field mice are found, and ask him to gather information for you about the field mice of his neighborhood, so you can compare notes on habits and habitats. The illustration in Figure 33 shows how this comparative information would be put into graphs and diagrams for your area. Ask for

similar data from your correspondent. See whether you can combine this information into a comparative graph.

Note that a careful record must be kept of activity in relation to rain and snowfall, sunshine, temperature, humidity, and growth of grass. You may note that one kind of mouse is most successful when it can dig tunnels under the snow. If the mouse had to live above the snow, it would need white protective coloration in wintertime like the snowshoe rabbit or like the mice that live in the white sands of New Mexico.

To get the most out of this comparative exploration you would probably need to compare your local mice with those in widely separated areas in order to come to various useful syntheses about meadow mice as a whole. But your first study with the naturalist in the other state would be a very useful beginning exercise.

(2) Study the leaf shapes and sizes across a section of an island, say Madagascar, as related to conditions of rainfall, altitude, shade, etc. that influence plant growth and adaptations, and compare these to leaf shapes and size in your neighborhood habitats. To carry out this rather exotic exploration you would need a good working knowledge of French, since French is the scientific language of this large island. You would need to contact, if possible, two or three or even four naturalists, amateur or professional, who live in a cross section across this island, and get them to send you actual pressed specimens of leaves, carefully giving the name of each bush or tree, something of its height and shape, and the exact location and time collected, and all information possible on the local climate and habitat.

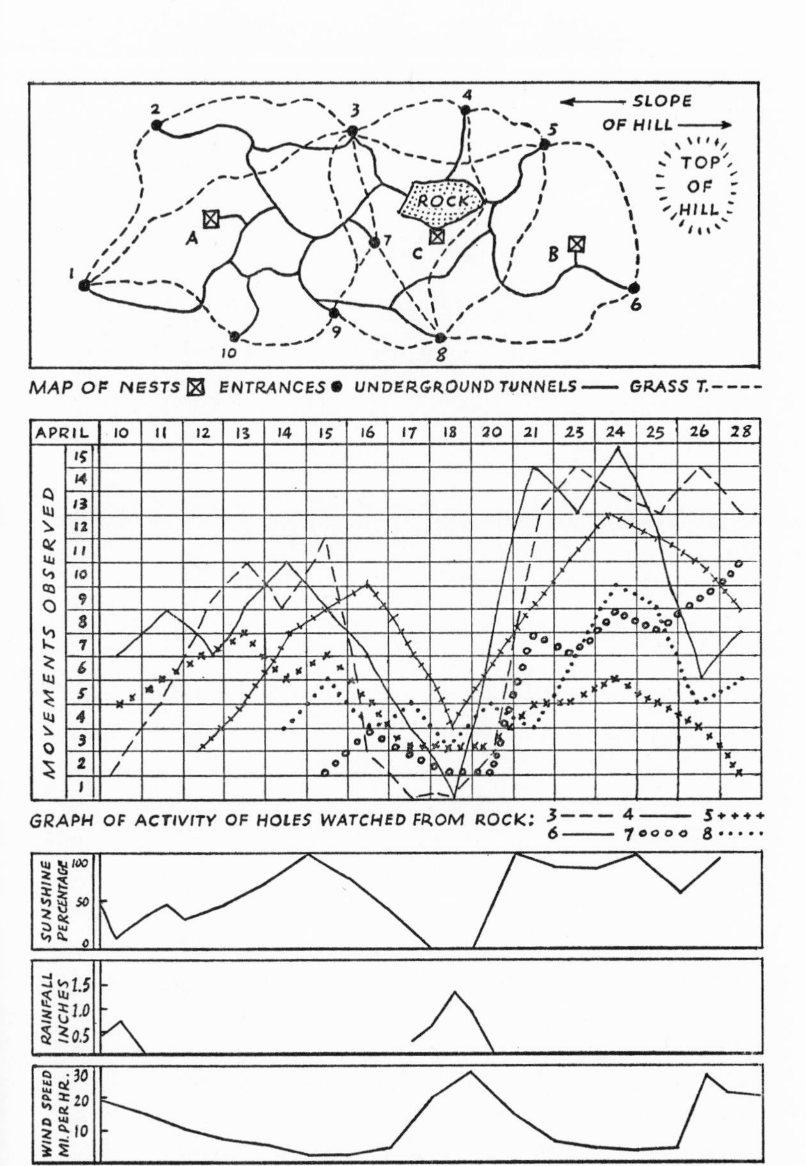

Fig. 33. Field Mouse Life: Map, Comparative Graphs and Diagrams

OBSERVATIONS MADE 5:30-6:00 A.M. EACH DAY. MAP MADE OF UNDERGROUND TUNNELS AT END OF EXPERIMENT.

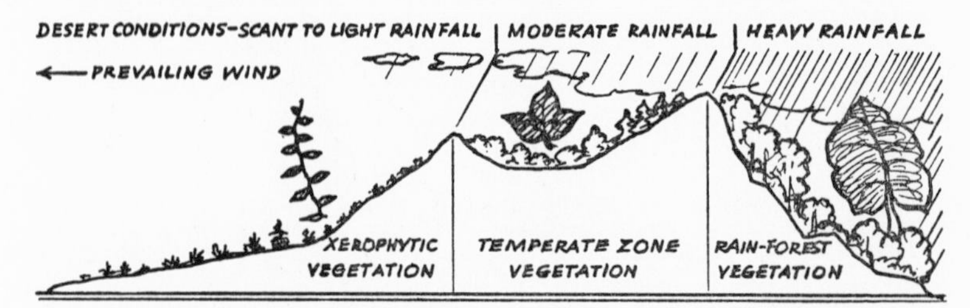

Fig. 34. Island Cross section Showing Relation of Leaf Types to Climates.

Arrange these pressed leaves on a chart on which you have diagrammed a cross section of the island. (NOTE: See Figure 34. This cross section is of an imaginary island, not Madagascar, as the facts on Madagascar are not at present available to me.) The cross section would be made from a contour map which you could find in a large library or send for from your state university library. On the cross section, indicate the different habitats wherever they are found as you cross the island, showing jungle, savanna, grassland, brushland, cultivated land, city and so forth. Then draw a red line from each leaf to the point on the cross section where that particular kind of plant is found. Below the cross section, show the average rainfall and temperature changes as you cross the island from one side to the other. This would show the connection between kind of climate and kind of leaf. Your synthesis would then be made to show the effects of the various habitat climates of the island on its plant cover.

Make a similar cross section chart of a stretch of geography in your own neighborhood and its varying types of leaves so you can make a comparison between your area and Madagascar. From many such comparisons, carefully and accurately done, scientists are able to work out the major laws of nature. What you do may be of help to them.

(3) Make a study of microclimates in your county as compared to a somewhat similar county in a state far away from where you are. For example, suppose you live in Marin County, California, which borders on both San Francisco Bay and the Pacific Ocean. You write to a fellow naturalist in Carteret County, North Carolina, which borders on both Pamlico Sound and the Atlantic Ocean, asking him to coöperate with you in such a study.

A microclimate is a small area with a special temperature and humidity range. It may have differences in precipitation and cloud cover from nearby areas. For example, scientists have found microclimates with a difference of as much as twenty degrees or more only a quarter of a mile apart on the same day. Differences in height above the ground also produce different microclimates, the temperature near the ground being different from that high in a tree. Humidity between such areas may also vary greatly. Thus, in one place with a microclimate of high temperature and high humidity semitropical trees such as oranges and avocados will flourish, while only a few hundred yards away it is always so cold that such trees die. A carefully kept map of the microclimates of your county, from week to week and month to month, after seeking out the causes of their differences (such as large buildings that cut off wind currents) may be of very great value to both scientists and local officials. Scientific zoning of housing and industrial developments should be done with close and careful consideration of microclimates. The reason for a comparative study of microclimates with a fellow naturalist in another part of the country is that both of you may gain information that will help you better understand your local microclimates and why they are formed. Be sure both you and your correspondent do as careful a job of mapping and studying as possible. The illustration in Figure 35 shows such a map of an imaginary area.

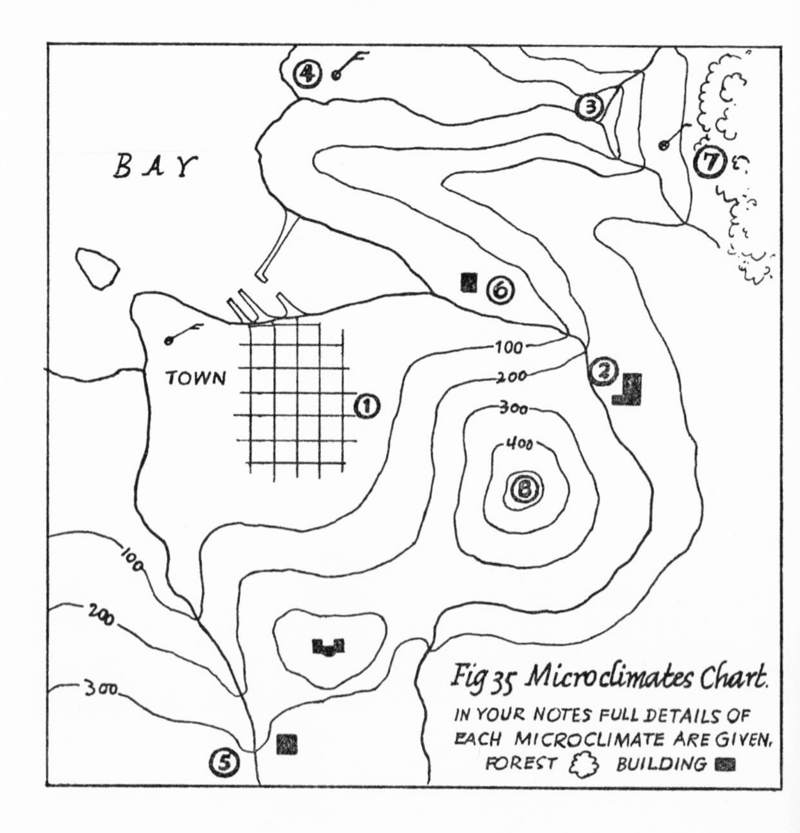

Fig 35 Microclimates Chart.

IN YOUR NOTES FULL DETAILS OF EACH MICROCLIMATE ARE GIVEN. FOREST BUILDING

Your friend in the other county will likely find microclimates that you do not seem to have, and you will probably find one or more he does not seem to have. Carefully note all the surrounding circumstances that appear to form them, such as wind direction, location in regard to nearby bodies of water, buildings, marshlands, forests, streams and contours of the land. See if similar conditions cannot be found in the opposing county and how close they come to producing the same microclimates.

To study you need six simple instruments (Figure 36): (*a*) a rain gauge (or more than one if you are testing rainfall in several places at once), (*b*) a thermometer

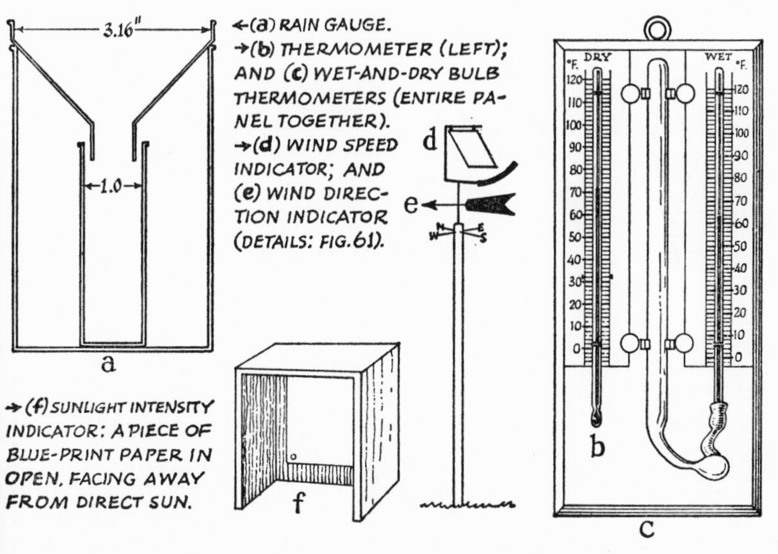

Fig. 36. Instruments Used to Study Microclimates.

to test varying temperatures; (*c*) a wet-and-dry bulb thermometer set for measuring humidity; (*d*) a wind gauge to test wind velocity, (*e*) a wind direction indicator, and (*f*) a simple sunlight indicator made with blue-print paper. All of these instruments and how to make them are described in any large encyclopedia and in *The Amateur Naturalist's Handbook*. Each instrument should be used at regular intervals at a number of different observation posts you have established throughout your county.

Sometimes you can find local amateurs who will be glad to help you maintain these separate stations and work with you on the mapping. Both temperature and humidity as well as wind direction and velocity should be tested at the surface of the ground, and also at different heights above the ground, since sometimes quite remarkable changes are found in a few feet. I can almost guarantee that you will be astonished at the many strange microclimates you will find in a small area and that, if you do the work carefully, you will be exploring a secret world of great value to mankind.

(4) Exchange seashells or rocks or minerals or insects with a naturalist in a foreign country, with the idea of comparing specimens by family or related families and by similar adaptations. For example, in your neighborhood you will find both insects and spiders that have adapted themselves for hiding in the insides of flowers and waiting there for an unwary bee or other flying insect that comes to sip the nectar. The animal hidden in the flower usually has colors that camouflage

Fig. 37. Crab Spider (LEFT) and Ambush Bug Wait for Insect Prey, on Flowers Which Give Camouflage Benefit.

its body to look like part of the flower. Suddenly it springs and grabs the insect that has just come flying in and quickly kills and eats it, usually by sucking out the body juices. Study all the kinds of insects and spiders in your neighborhood that do this kind of ambushing and take notes on exactly how they do it, including drawings to show the whole process. Send specimens of these insects and spiders to your friend in a foreign country (we will say in Chile), describing what these creatures do, and asking him to send back similar species from his neighborhood with full descriptions of how they catch their prey.

This, of course, is just a beginning, though a valuable one. If you spread this study to other parts of the earth, after awhile you may put together in your laboratory the living creatures themselves and their prey, simulating so far as possible the natural conditions of their homelands. Such a study may give you information of real worth in combatting insect pests.

The greatest values of all in contacting foreign lands and distant states and provinces come from widening your horizons and from giving you increasingly intimate views into the lives of animals and plants of distant countries — and also into the lives of distant people.

6

SECRET WORLDS UNDER THE GROUND

PERHAPS no secret worlds contain so many treasures as the worlds under the ground. The metals and minerals that form the core of our civilization were discovered underground, as were dazzling gems, and a great variety of chemicals used in industry and in the home. Among other treasure found in this way should be included the wonderful earthworm, who creates new soil, and the rivers of underground water that can be tapped to irrigate deserts.

The mystery and excitement of underground exploring comes from working often in complete ignorance of what is ahead of you, then suddenly breaking through to some great new surprise. There is no need to remind you that such work has its dangers. Old mines, for example, should not be entered unless experts declare them completely safe; even then, young people should be accompanied by adults and every precaution should be taken to explore with safety.

When I was a young and untrained explorer of underground worlds I did everything wrong about such exploring. I am lucky to be alive after taking so much risk and danger! I went with a couple of other young fellows to explore an old epsomite mine near Oakland, California. This mine had many other interesting minerals in it besides the white epsomite from which Epsom salts are made, including red melanterite and the very lovely feathery blue boothite.

The first thing we did wrong was to enter the mine without telling anybody where we were going. This was a very serious mistake, If a cave-in had trapped us inside the mine, no one would have known where to look for us.

Our second mistake was in climbing beyond an old cave-in. About sixty feet in from the mine entrance the roof had caved in, leaving a large pile of dirt and rocks on the floor, over which we crawled. But this was a warning that another similar and probably worse cave-in would come at any time. After feeling our way with our flashlights for about two hundred feet along a dark tunnel, we came to a shaft going straight down into the bowels of the earth, with a wooden ladder allowing a way to climb down.

"Shall we try it?" asked Denny.

"Yes!" said I, and boldly and foolishly led the way down into those dark depths, for mistake number three. I had not climbed down ten feet before a rotten crosspiece gave way under my foot, my hand jerked free from the rung above, and I felt myself falling down through darkness! Wildly I grabbed at a ladder rung. Fortunately the wood was sound and my sudden fall was brought short with a sickening lurch. Far below I heard the tinkling crash as my flashlight hit the bottom of the shaft.

Our third mistake was followed by our fourth. Instead of turning back at this point, we used the remaining two flashlights to explore down the ladder, carefully feeling each step of the way for rotten crossbars, until we came to two side tunnels into which we crawled to look for minerals. In one of these we found what looked like a real fairy cavern, a place whose walls were lined with sparkling boothite, its feathery texture aglow like soft blue satin in the beams of our lights. Some of this and other minerals we brought to the surface, but I can still remember the horror that swept through me when I read in the newspapers a month later that the very mine we had explored had completely caved in!

Exploring under the earth does not always mean going into mines or caves. Turning over a rock to see what is underneath, breaking a rock through the middle, exploring quarries, fresh road-cuts or ravines, are other ways of seeing what is under the surface of this earth. Many an untrained man has unknowingly kicked aside dirty brown rocks that actually carried hidden treasures of beautiful crystals or rare minerals inside the common-looking exteriors. The explorer breaks open such rocks to see what is inside, and tests what he finds there to see if it is valuable or has meaning.

PLANTS UNDER THE EARTH

The only plants that appear to live completely in darkness under the earth are certain fungi, bacteria and viruses. Take any cubic inch of soil and look at it carefully, part by part under a high-powered microscope. You will

Fig. 38. Mycelia of Fungi are the Plants, not Root Systems. THE MUSHROOMS ABOVE GROUND ARE THE FRUIT-BODIES.

Fig. 39. Mesquite Roots May Reach 100 ft. to Water Beneath the Desert Floor.

be astonished at the number of soil bacteria you will find there. Often there are also the mycelia of fungi, ghostly threads that stretch their all but invisible fingers down and down through the darkness. Viruses are also found there, so tiny that only the most powerful and expensive microscopes show them to us.

This plant life within the soil, sometimes found even in the cracks of rocks or in their hearts when moisture has oozed in, can be only explored by a microscope and by countless testings and siftings. You try to find out what kinds of soil grow what kinds of bacteria and fungi, and how they may affect the growth and health of the larger plants that root in such soil. From such studies comes a knowledge of soils that may increase the crops of the farmer and also show him how and where to produce plants that are resistant to diseases.

Classifying bacteria and fungi is necessary in order to understand which ones are helpful and which are harmful. Books listed at the back of this book will help you do this. Write notes on the effects of the different kinds of bacteria and fungi on the soils in which you find them. Soils themselves are classified according to how much clay, iron, sand, humus and various other materials or chemicals are found in them. Books on soils will help you classify them.

Figure 40 shows how the results of an exploration of soil bacteria and fungi can be synthesized in a graph and diagram that tells the story of a particular type of soil. Notice the importance of nitrogen-producing bacteria, which are stimulated only by certain plants such as beans, in developing a rich soil. Notice also that too rich a bacteria-count in the soil can limit plant growth.

A whole battery of secret worlds can be explored when you take up the study of different plant roots. Some roots are very shallow and the plants that have them may live only a few months or even weeks during the rainy season. Other roots reach so deep into the earth that even in a hot and dry desert they may find water over a hundred feet beneath the surface of the earth (Figure 39). How each kind of plant uses and develops its root system for its own good is a world to explore in itself. How roots hold the soil, how too many roots may severely lower the water table, how roots may be used

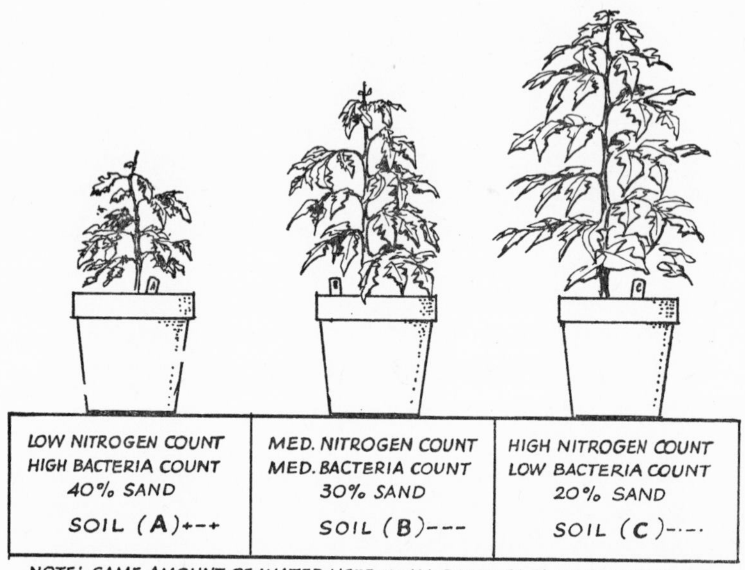

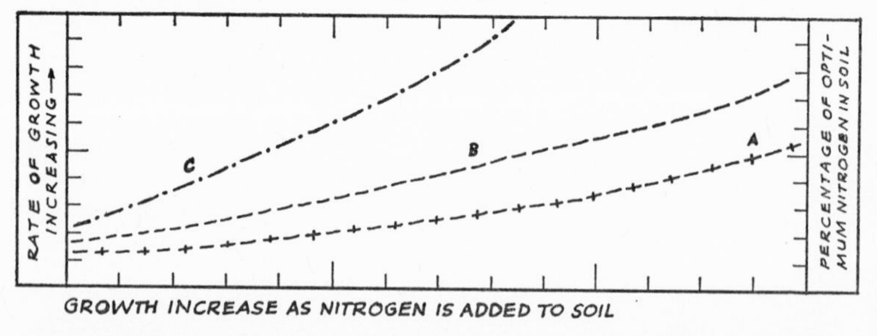

Fig. 40. Relation of Nitrogen and Bacteria in Soil to Plant Growth. A QUANTITATIVE EXPERIMENT (RESULTS SHOWN ARE HYPOTHETICAL SAMPLE).

by plants as weapons of war in overcoming and driving out other plants from favorite localities, and how roots can be used as a protection against fires are but a few of the other explorations that can be made on this subject.

The diagram shows how roots may be studied to learn how much water each different plant is drawing from the soil (Figure 41). During a year's time you could make a scientific exploration of how the roots in your garden are taking up moisture. If you can put a meter on the hose that waters this particular garden and keep an accurate rain gauge, you can determine approximately the total amount of water given to the garden during a definite period. Compare this to the number of plants in the garden, and carefully measure the amount of water

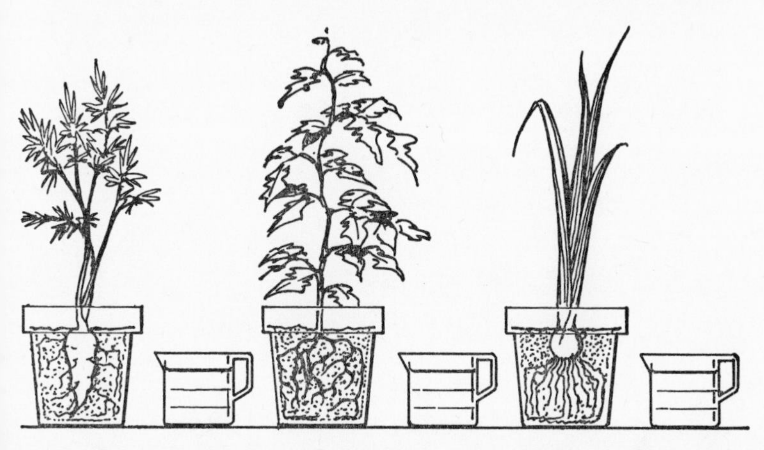

Fig. 41. Varying Amounts of Water Drawn from Soil by Different Types of Roots: EXAMPLES—SMALL ROOTS (TOMATO); THICK TAPROOT (CARROT); & BULB (ONION). TAKE IDENTICAL POTS; FILL WITH SAME WEIGHT OF SOIL; ADD SAME QUANTITY OF WATER AT SAME TIME. KEEP TOPS OF POTS COVERED TIGHTLY WITH FOIL TO PREVENT SOIL-AIR INTAKE OR LOSS OF WATER.

PROCEDURE: WITH ALL THREE PLANTS IN COMPARABLE DEVELOPMENT, WEIGH EACH ONE CAREFULLY; ADD SAME AMOUNT OF WATER TO EACH; WAIT 24 HOURS; THEN WEIGH CAREFULLY AGAIN TO DETERMINE—

taken up on the average each day by each kind of plant. This can be done by measuring water evaporation in each kind of plant (as shown in Figure 42) by weighing each pot at twenty-four-hour intervals (knowing the weight of water added each day). From such information the efficiency of the plants in your garden can be determined. Some root systems are better adapted to your climate and soil and the amount of water given than others.

EXPLORING ANIMALS UNDER THE EARTH

One day when I was digging an underground cellar and was down about eight feet, I was annoyed to notice that little bunches of dirt were falling down one place on the wall. Finally I went over to watch and quickly saw

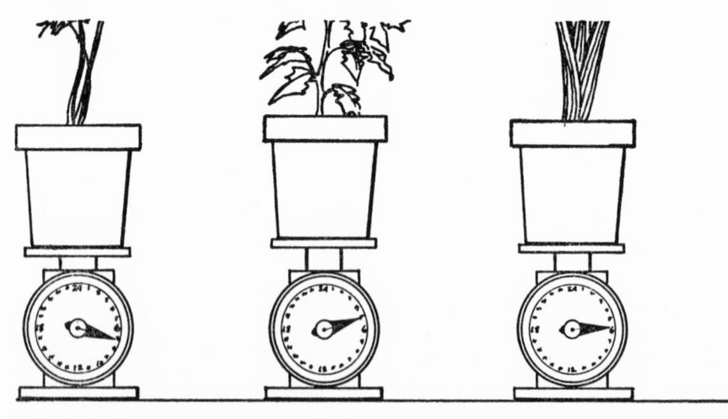

Fig. 42. Water Evaporation Through Leaves of Plants.

VARIABLES AND UNKNOWNS TO FIND THROUGH FURTHER EXPERIMENTATION: (1) RELATIVE EVAPORATION THROUGH DIFFERENT TYPES OF LEAVES. (2) LEAF-ROOT RATIO. (3) EFFECT OF TEMPERATURE, HUMIDITY, ETC.

that up near the top of the wall there was a small hole. Soon some dirt was pushed out of this hole and fell to the bottom of the digging. Then out poked a little brown nose and two black beady eyes that looked down at me apparently without recognizing that I was a human being, since I was standing still. It was the face of Botta Pocket Gopher. The animal had been delighted to find a wonderful place to dump the dirt out of its underground tunnels. Instead of struggling to get it above ground into the usual gopher mound, where there was always the danger of being caught by a hawk or a cat, all this wise gopher had to do was to shove his dirt straight out a level hole into a beautifully convenient garbage dump!

I watched this gopher many times dumping its dirt and, as long as I stood still, it would proceed without paying any attention to me. The life of the gopher has been studied comparatively little and it has occurred to me that it could be studied more with the use of red-light windows and special signals set inside the gopher tunnels. Since gophers do a vast amount of damage every year to flower and vegetable gardens and are also responsible for undermining irrigation ditches and even dams across creeks, such a study might be of considerable value to man.

Here I should like to make the point that for you to get into the habit of exploring secret worlds mainly because you think you can discover something of value to mankind may make you a poor scientist. Scientists do a great deal of what is called "basic research," a large part of which may be considered useless by the so-called practical man. Yet this research is vital to the increase of overall knowledge. Furthermore, exploring the unknown for the pure pleasure of exploring should not be spoiled by constant worry about the practical value of this or that exploration.

Like most animals, gophers are comparatively insensible to red light. By putting red-glass windows along the tops of gopher tunnels, the little animals could be watched at their underground work. Such windows could also be put along the sides of an artificial gopher tunnel, like that illustrated in (Figure 43), in which the walls of glass are only about four inches apart. In such an artificial tunnel, the gopher could be watched from both

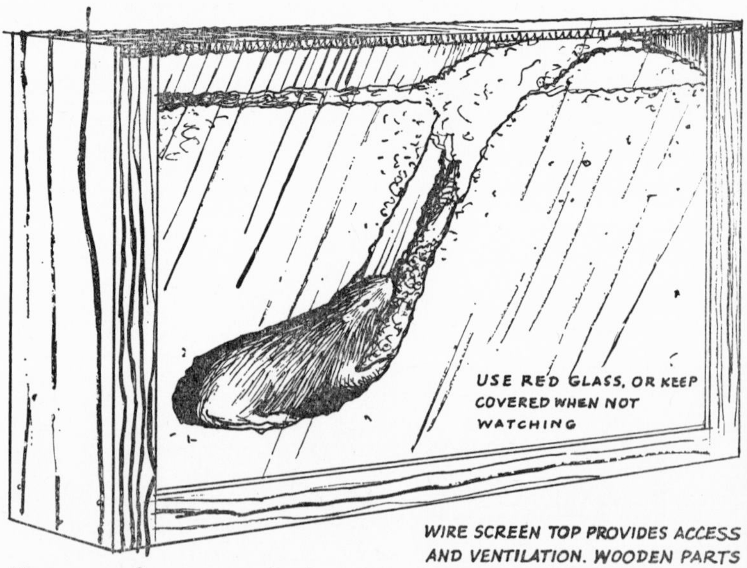

Fig. 43. Gopher Cage with Glass Sides.

sides and could never get out of sight. However, I should warn that when a friend of mine tried an artificial tunnel of this kind the gopher soon died. Something was wrong — probably too much humidity between the glass walls. This is something you would have to overcome.

Signal trip wires set in a gopher tunnel would ring a buzzer when the gopher had passed that way, or even record its passing on a revolving drum. From this graphs could be made. One might show just how often in each twenty-four hour period a gopher passed a given point in his tunnel. Or by careful day-by-day observation, you could also determine how many new tunnel openings a

Fig. 44. Graph of Gopher Activities. June-July: 5:30-6 A.M.

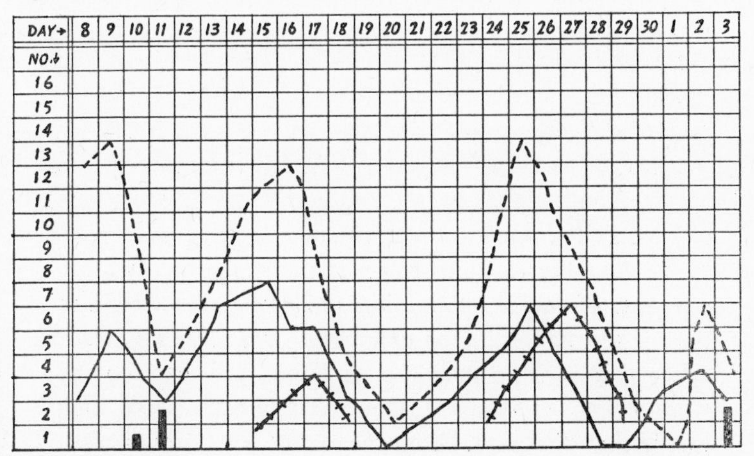

gopher makes in a day (Figure 44) and then plot them on a map along with a diagram showing the extent and nature of the gopher's activity. This latter map could be made after digging out a complete circuit of the gopher's tunnels; quite a job, but good exercise!

Limestone caves, lava caves, and often old mines are hiding and living places for bats, amphibians, strange insects and sometimes even fish. The scientific explorer of such caves is called a "speleologist," and there are speleologist organizations in many states and provinces. It is wise to join such an organization to carry out cave explorations, because the men and women who conduct them are usually thoroughly experienced and take every precaution to see that each member of a cave expedition comes back alive.

There are many worlds within worlds to explore in these caves, but the first of all things to do in cave exploration is to prepare a map of the cave (See Figure 45). A cord or fishline, marked off in feet, is a necessary tool for this exploration, or a fifty-foot tape measure is even better. Another tool needed is a compass. As you enter a cave start measuring direction and length of each part of it from the entranceway. Take a sighting with the compass of the first direction the cave takes and mark this in a notebook (for example, "NW 320 degrees"). After this is done measure as far as you can go in a straight line and mark this in the notebook as so many feet in that direction. From the end of your first measurement, take a new sighting and make a new measurement. Measure also the width and height of the cave at each such stopping place, and the angle at which you travel

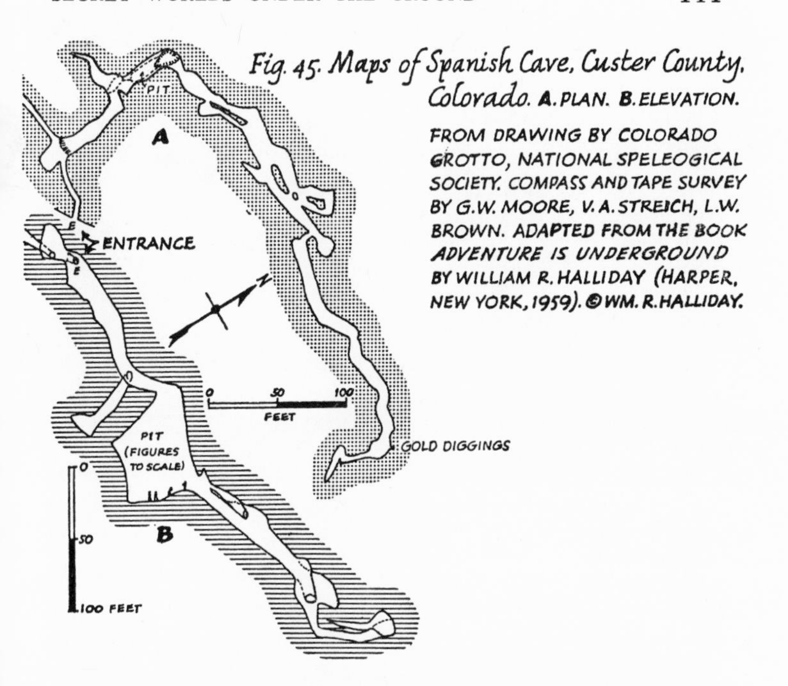

Fig. 45. Maps of Spanish Cave, Custer County, Colorado. A. PLAN. B. ELEVATION.

FROM DRAWING BY COLORADO GROTTO, NATIONAL SPELEOGICAL SOCIETY. COMPASS AND TAPE SURVEY BY G.W. MOORE, V.A. STREICH, L.W. BROWN. ADAPTED FROM THE BOOK *ADVENTURE IS UNDERGROUND* BY WILLIAM R. HALLIDAY (HARPER, NEW YORK, 1959). © WM. R. HALLIDAY.

up or down. When you have finished exploring the cave, all this data in your notebook can be translated into a map as shown. You will note that you can actually make maps of the cave, a horizontal one and a series of vertical cross sections (shown on the second map). This gives a total picture of the cave and where it goes.

Other useful instruments include a wet-and-dry bulb thermometer, so that you can measure both temperature and humidity in different parts of the cave, marking these temperatures and humidity percentages both in your notes and on the map. To determine directions of air currents in different parts of the cave wet your finger and hold it up. The cool side of the finger will be the side from which the current of air is blowing. These air currents may help you discover other entranceways to the cave. Of course a good supply of matches and candles for emergency should be taken into the cave besides your flashlight and a supply of extra batteries and globes.

During the mapping of the cave you will discover various animals in different places. The exact locality in which each species is found should be put in both your notes and on the map. It can be done on the map by using a number for each animal, the number being repeated with the name in your notebook. Be sure your records of the temperature, humidity and wind currents at each place are as accurate as possible. Gradually you will begin to put together the facts about the total animal life found in the cave, and from this, in time, you can make your syntheses or conclusions as to how, why and where animals live in the cave and how they have especially adapted themselves to it. If an underground stream runs through the cave, you are in luck — because many creatures, such as blind fish and blind salamanders, may live in its waters. To catch them a long-handled net is almost certainly needed. Never catch any more than necessary of any one kind of animal, but take careful notes on all you see. (How to catch, preserve and mount specimens is explained in *The Amateur Naturalist's Handbook.*)

A lava cave I explored and mapped in the jungles of western Panama was literally alive with all kinds of strange life. Holes in the roof of the cave were so filled with hundreds and hundreds of bats of at least five different species that, when disturbed, the roaring sound of their wings was like the roar of a great underground waterfall. As we entered the cave and our voices aroused them, every square inch of air soon seemed filled with flying forms. They brushed against us and rushed out into the daylight, but even when these great numbers were gone, we still found many hundreds more hidden up in the roof tunnels. By shaking nets against these places, we captured all we needed for our study.

On the walls huge pseudo-scorpions, some of them as much as four inches long, crawled about searching for bat lice and other small creatures on which they fed. Their ferocious-looking chelicerae, pincers, waved savagely above their heads, but when I tried to capture them, they rushed off in great fright. Nevertheless several good specimens were netted. After a two hundred yard penetration of the cave, my assistant left me to take out the bats we had captured, while I went on alone. Deep in the cave I began to notice that a bat was following me, squeaking angrily. At the end of the main part of the cave she lit on a rock above my head and glared down at me as if to say "What's the idea catching us bats in that net?" I didn't pay too much attention to her until she suddenly let go her hold and flew straight down to my thumb, on which she lighted for an instant and gave one hard bite that startled me more than it hurt me. With a cry, I flung her away into the darkness and heard her squeak of triumph as she rushed off down the cavern!

A wind current against my wet finger made me believe that the cave had another entranceway, but when I started down a narrow side tunnel through which the current blew, I had an uneasy feeling of danger. Gradually the ceiling got lower and lower until I was forced first to move forward on my hands and knees, watching out carefully as I moved for scorpions and poisonous snakes, and then finally on my stomach. At last I saw roots coming down through the roof, and I squeezed past this narrow point with a grunt of effort and wormed my way into a most delightful room where soft light came from a bush and vine-covered entranceway.

A loud spitting noise exploded in front of me and my flashlight's beam caught the reflection of two fiery yellow eyes. I shouted, partly in fear and partly to frighten this sudden underground enemy. With a savage growl, a large ocelot or tiger cat sprang out through the entranceway and disappeared. I was very fortunate that there were no young ocelots in the cave, for, if there had been, I am sure the parent would have attacked me.

In this final room I found not only plenty of signs of ocelots living there, including many bones of small animals and birds, but also jungle mice that lived in tunnels in the walls where the ocelots could not catch them, salamanders that hid under trash on the floor, and many kinds of insects, including almost blind cave crickets, numerous beetles and flies that fed on both the dung and old meat and bones of the ocelots, as well as other beetles, that fed on the dung-eaters.

MINERALS, ROCKS AND FOSSILS UNDER THE EARTH

River and stream beds, cuts in rocks made by streams, old mines, quarries, limestone caves, road cuts, cliffs, lava flows and similar places lead you into the worlds of rocks, minerals and fossils. Good geology and fossil books, such as those mentioned in the back of this book, are necessary for understanding rock formations and identifying what you find. These can be secured at most libraries.

Most people who collect rocks and minerals do so with little purpose or merely to find pretty things for a collection or for jewelry. The true explorer singles out some particular problem of the underearth world that is either not understood or only partly understood. Then he begins to unravel the secrets of this problem by careful investigation, study and research.

Here are some suggested explorations:

(1) Explore how salts are carried in solution under the earth and deposited in the inner parts of rocks and elsewhere. We know, of course, that hot water carries such salts in much larger quantities than cold water. This can be seen if you visit Yellowstone National Park or anywhere that hot water geysers and springs deposit great quantities of salts. If you live near such a place and can obtain permission from the owners of a geyser or hot spring, perhaps you can do some of your experimenting with hot water and salts under natural conditions. Other-

wise you have to try to duplicate the conditions artificially with pyrex beakers and test tubes. Running hot water through a long test tube to a pottery vessel kept cold with ice or some other method of refrigeration will show you just how many salts are deposited (Figure 46).

Keep careful records and graphs to show at what temperature and what percentage various salts go into solution and at what temperature they are deposited. The direction your exploration will take will depend a good deal on what happens with the different salts and the different mixtures of salts you try. You may find a combination with reactions that produce quite spectacular or unusual results. Take any salts you find in nature to a chemical laboratory to be analyzed. If a valuable salt is found, it would be worth your while to try to discover

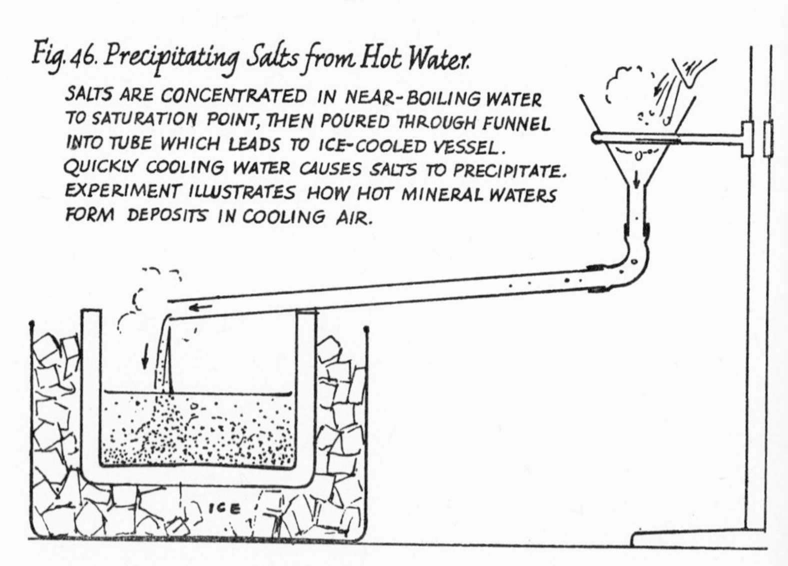

Fig. 46. Precipitating Salts from Hot Water.

SALTS ARE CONCENTRATED IN NEAR-BOILING WATER TO SATURATION POINT, THEN POURED THROUGH FUNNEL INTO TUBE WHICH LEADS TO ICE-COOLED VESSEL. QUICKLY COOLING WATER CAUSES SALTS TO PRECIPITATE. EXPERIMENT ILLUSTRATES HOW HOT MINERAL WATERS FORM DEPOSITS IN COOLING AIR.

how nature produced it by trying to repeat the same conditions in your laboratory or in nature.

(2) Select an interesting or valuable mineral that is found in your county and thoroughly explore its distribution, its associates and everything else that pertains to how and where it is found. This is one of the most exciting of all underearth explorations, because it may actually lead to hidden treasure. Suppose you take as your subject the beautiful blue-green copper ore called malachite. Malachite itself, unless found in considerable quantity, has only limited value, but it is a weathered vein ore, which means it appears on the surface as an indicator of other and more valuable copper ores that may underlie a find of malachite. Malachite is usually found associated with certain other minerals, such as native copper, chalcocite, azurite, chrysocolla, bornite, cuprite and limonite. But in your county perhaps only some of these and perhaps some other minerals may be indicated by the presence of malachite. This can be found out first by a study of all available records of the presence of malachite in your county and the minerals found with it, and second from some good hard exploration of your own. You would visit all the known malachite deposits and copper mines in your county and see the relation at such places of malachite to other minerals. Then, as you hiked over the county, you would look for similar conditions elsewhere that might lead to a malachite and copper ore discovery. If you make such a discovery, ask your state Bureau of Mines for advice as to what to do about it.

In the state of California where I live gold has always been a mineral for which men searched most carefully.

Yet one of the best ways to search for gold has not been used as frequently as others. Many of the ancient gold-bearing streams in the Sierra Nevadas, particularly the northern Sierras, were covered over, ages ago, by outpourings of lava erruptions. As the lava hardened into rock, it completely covered and hid the gold-bearing gravels of the streams over which the hot liquid lava had flowed. Today, by exploring carefully along the edges of lava outcroppings and digging down wherever there are low exposures of the lava, you have the chance of locating some of these ancient gold-bearing gravels. Such exploration can also be very fruitful scientifically too, because in these ancient stream beds are sometimes found rare and valuable fossils, as well as unusual minerals other than gold.

(3) Join the search for fossils. Fossils are a key to the ancient history of the earth and what has lived here in past ages. But they are often delicate things, easily destroyed by the careless collector, and, of course, fossils collected without scientific notes or labels and stuffed

Fig. 47. An Easily-built Sluice Box.

away in closets are perfectly useless to science. Wherever you find any, carefully put down in your notebook the exact location and time. Put numbers with your notes and paint similar numbers (quite small) on the fossils (Figure 48). The number may be painted on with a fine brush with either black or white enamel paint, using the color that will stand out best against the color of the fossil.

If you are so lucky as to find a large or small fossil bed, you have before you a most exciting world to explore and one that can be of great scientific value. Find a good book on fossils and fossil collecting before you start exploring. (See books listed at end of this book.) If you take your specimens, and samples also of the rock in

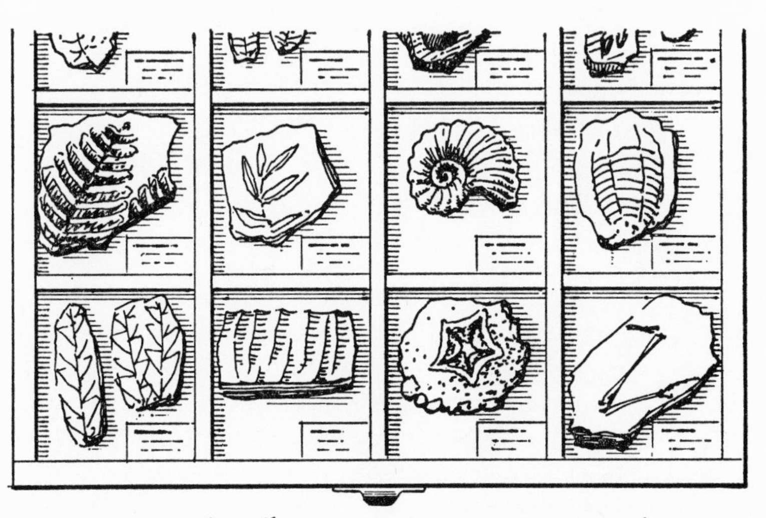

Fig. 48. A Sample Collection of Various Types of Fossils.

which they are found as well as good photographs of the fossil location, to your nearest paleontological museum, they can usually tell you what strata and age of rocks you have found your fossils in. With this knowledge, you can then turn to the large books in their library (or obtain such books through your local library) and find out just what is known about that age and rock strata and the fossils that have so far been found in it. With this knowledge you are then ready to go on with your own exploration. Gradually you will uncover many fossils already found, but, if you are lucky, you may encounter new or rare ones of scientific interest. As you go on and on with your digging and findings, you may have the opportunity to develop your own syntheses from the different facts you uncover in one fossil bed, as has been done in the sample map (Figure 49). Such a map should certainly be made of your exploration, along with cross-section diagrams and graphs that help bring out the story of what happened in that place long ago.

ANCIENT RUINS AND THE REMAINS OF ANCIENT MEN

The science of archaeology often involves as much digging and rock-cutting as does the hunt for fossils (paleontology). There is always the chance of finding a lost treasure, some ancient artifact or skeleton of value. Unfortunately too many careless hunters in the past have destroyed more than they have found. To be a scientific explorer for ancient remains of men and their buildings and artifacts means taking the greatest care not to cover

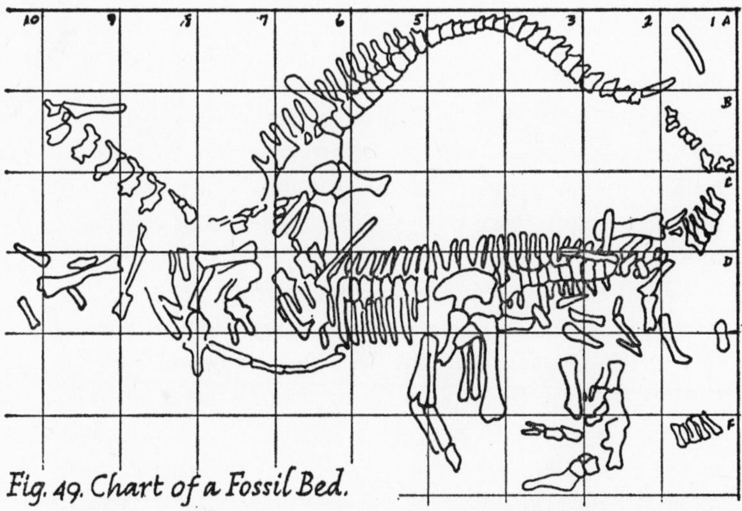

Fig. 49. Chart of a Fossil Bed.

THE EXPOSED SURFACE OF THE BED IS CAREFULLY CLEANED AND THE BONES NUMBERED TO KEY THEM TO THE CHART WHICH ENABLES THE PALEONTOLOGIST TO PUT THEM WHERE THEY BELONG WHEN MAKING A RECONSTRUCTION LATER ON IN THE LABORATORY. (MODIFIED FROM *THE DOUBLEDAY PICTORIAL LIBRARY OF NATURE.*)

an important find, or destroy it. It is easy to handle things so carelessly as to break or otherwise mar them, and it is, of course, very easy to forget to take notes. But everything found must be handled as if it were priceless porcelain, each separate piece being carefully marked with a number, and then a very complete description written down telling exactly where and how it was found and any other useful details about it. A photograph or even several photographs should be taken of its position when found.

On Cocos Island in the Pacific Ocean off Costa Rica so many foolish treasure hunters have come looking for the pirate treasure supposedly hidden there that they have almost completely ruined the island and made it more and more unlikely that the treasure will ever be found. They have done this by digging all over the place without any intelligent plan of attack and especially by bulldozing huge quantities of dirt into great piles that probably totally hide any possible evidence of the treasure.

In Panama I was fortunate enough to be present when two trained archaeologists found some of the lost treasure of the Doraske Indians. We had all been searching for this treasure by looking for ancient Indian *guacos,* or graves. These graves are usually marked with mounds of rocks, but often such a mound would become covered over with several layers of jungle soil. To find the graves we would stick long steel spikes down through the soft dirt, probing about in hopes of hitting something solid. The two archaeologists were fortunate enough to hit with their probes the stones of a chief's grave. By digging down some twenty feet, they finally came to some large pottery urns, several strangely shaped into the forms of tigers, monkeys and crocodiles. In some of these urns were the beautiful silver and gold ornaments the Doraske Indians had made. There were solid gold horns, bracelets, necklaces, and also queer figurines of Indian heads with eagle-winged headdresses. There were also gold tigers, eagles, monkeys and snakes, and one complete six-inch-high skeleton of a man, made of gold!

I noticed that the scientists were extremely careful about everything they found. An accurate map was made of the whole area, and another map of the find. As soon as the grave was opened, it was photographed several times. Then each piece that was taken out was carefully numbered and placed on a white cloth where it was again photographed. The dirt was removed from every object with the utmost care and every precaution was taken to see that nothing was broken. All the time their busy pens were writing down everything they saw or thought about each discovery as they found it, so there would be little chance of anything being missed. Later all these things would be put in a great museum and would be studied in comparison with similar archaeological finds from other areas, as the scientists worked to reveal the story of this ancient civilization.

Before that, when I was a young fellow, I had taken part in digging out several Indian mounds along the edge of San Francisco Bay. I am sorry to admit that most of the skeletons and the stone and bone tools we found then are now scattered among several families with no records of where they came from, or how deep in the dirt they were found. When you do your exploring of ancient ruins, please do your best to do the job as those real scientists did and not as a careless amateur. In the one case something can be added to mankind's knowledge. In the other, something priceless may be lost.

WARNING: There is a national law against the digging up of archaeological finds in the United States without proper permission. It is usually not possible to obtain this permission unless you can prove that you are a qualified student of archaeology. It is best for you to work with the archaeology department of your nearest university or your nearest historical society in searching for and digging up archaeological finds, thus making sure that their value is not lost to society. Convince them that you are really interested and want to help in the right way and under proper supervision. These organizations particularly need such help when an area of countryside where archaeological finds might be found is about to be covered by a reservoir or to be destroyed by buildings or new highways. Then many careful diggers are needed.

7

SECRET WORLDS UNDER WATER

SKIN DIVERS are thronging our coasts to explore beneath the surface of the sea, drawn by the urge for adventure and fun. Gradually some of the more serious among them are turning to scientific exploration of the life under the sea. They have only just begun their search for the secret worlds to be found there.

Sailing among rocky islets off the coast of Indo China near the small anthracite coal mining port of Kamfa long ago I could see beneath the clear waters riots of color among sea animals and plants of such indescribable beauty I longed to swim down among them. But I could not leave the ship on which I was working, and so had no chance to explore that paradise. Since that time I have explored beautiful undersea gardens along the coasts of Panama and California. Down under the water your body slips through cool green lights and shadows, through waving fern-like fronds of seaweed, over beds of tentacle-waving green, gray or blue sea anemones; then, above, the red, pulsating banks of giant sea urchins, and the rhythmically swaying gardens of sea pens and sea hydroids. You feel yourself in a lost fairy world, far removed from the dusty, noisy, smelly earth of city man.

With equal joy I have lain on the bank of a quiet country stream and peered for hours into the clear waters, watching the water insects and spiders, the water worms and other creatures wandering among the forests of water plants, carrying out the ceaseless drama of hunt and be hunted, escape and kill and eat. But watching is not enough. The real joy comes from discovering things never before seen by man. To do this takes, first, study and research to find out what is known already; then, careful explorations for the unknown. Here are some suggested explorations:

(1) Why not put a window on the side of a pond, as suggested in Chapter 1, so you can watch the pond life at different levels and see what differences there are? You can build a waterproof box with a long sealed window along one side and lower this into a square hole you have dug in the side of the pond, using braces stuck in the dirt to hold it down (Figure 50). Crouched in this diving

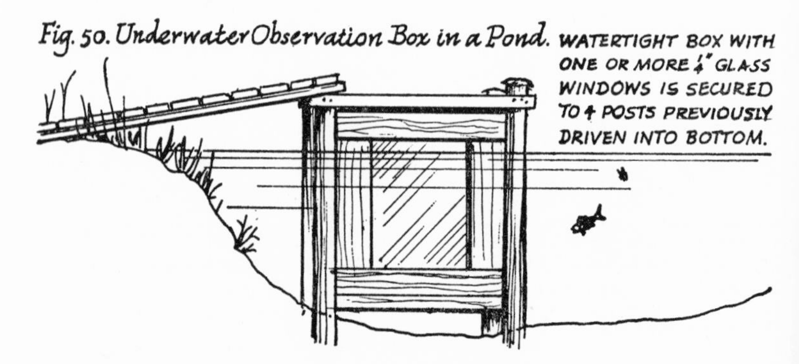

Fig. 50. Underwater Observation Box in a Pond. WATERTIGHT BOX WITH ONE OR MORE 1/4" GLASS WINDOWS IS SECURED TO 4 POSTS PREVIOUSLY DRIVEN INTO BOTTOM.

bell you can comfortably watch the life under water. The glass window will gradually become a part of the pond, water plants will grow up in front of it, and water animals come to stare in at you or go about their business. By dropping fish food into the water in front of the window and sitting very still, you can attract many creatures to this part of the pond and observe their actions.

The temperature of the water should be recorded two or three times a day and you should also notice the effect of sunlight and shadow upon the water life. Keep a graph such as that in Figure 51, which will show the relation between the activity of the water animals and tempera-

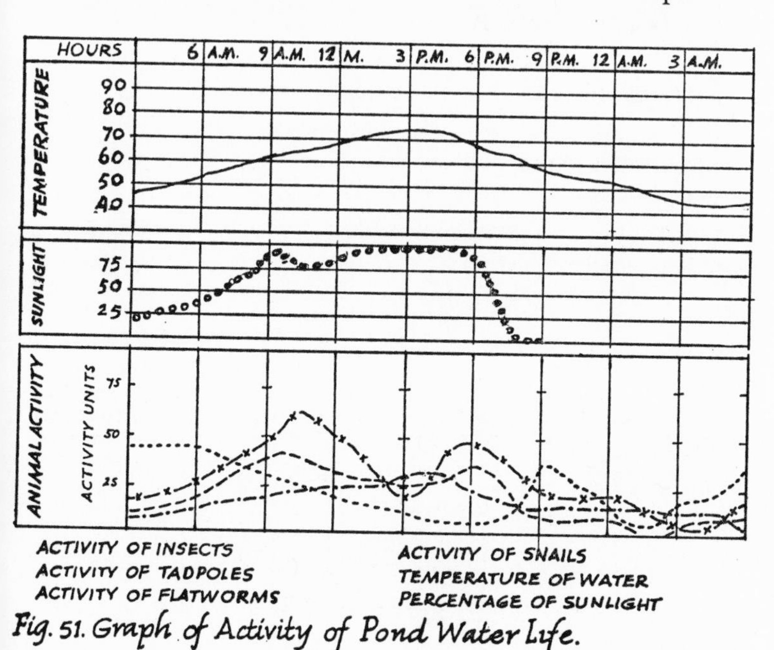

Fig. 51. Graph of Activity of Pond Water Life.

ture and sunlight. At night you can flash a red light into the water, or, better still, drop a waterproof cord and waterproof bulb into the water in front of your window so that you can watch night activity. Record in your notebook everything that happens by night or day. Particularly note the differences in life at different levels: one foot, two feet, three feet and so on. Of course the deeper down your underwater window goes the more variety of life you will see. There is no telling what secrets of the underwater life you may discover!

(2) One of the most interesting of all creatures to study under fresh water is the crayfish. There is considerable character variation among crayfish and they do many funny things. I remember one big crayfish that came up to nibble at my toe. It seemed to dislike the taste, because it suddenly backed away, made a complete flip around and started throwing sand at my toe with its tail!

If you put crayfish into an aquarium, don't expect other creatures to live with them. The crayfish are usually quite hungry and soon eat up whatever they can catch. It is better simply to keep them to themselves, unless you

Fig. 52. Crayfish Throwing Sand.

wish to feed them live animals. Feed them meat regularly every day, taking out any that is left over after a meal so it will not decay in the water. While some things can be learned about them in captivity and certainly you should keep careful day-by-day records, it is far better to watch them in their natural environment. You can do this partly by the sunken window method already described, but to see the action of a single crayfish over a long period of time you need to follow it about, preferably with a glass-bottomed box or pail in order to see its actions more clearly. If you wade through the water very slowly and carefully, moving only when the crayfish's eyes are facing away from you, you can probably follow it without disturbing the animal itself. You can see how it deals with enemies, how it gets along with other crayfish, and how it captures its food. Make a careful map to show the route it follows, and diagrams of its various actions along the way.

The key to learning vital secrets about the life of the crayfish, just as with other animals, is a combination of patience with a strong desire to learn all you can about the animal. Gradually, from following the crayfish about, you begin to feel close to them and at last can even sense their feelings and reactions. Soon you may discover what no man has seen before. When you do, take notes on all you see. If you can take photographs, that is better still.

(3) A stream, particularly a swift stream, has very different life from that of a pond. Exploring such a stream you need carefully to turn over rocks under the water and catch and watch what is on the underside.

Some naturalists put a wide net across a stream and then walk upstream turning over rocks. Animals loosened by this activity float down into the net. Many animals, such as caddis worms, cling to the undersides of rocks and put forth their own nets to catch whatever tiny food the water brings to them. Perhaps you could arrange an ingenious underwater mirror such as that shown in Figure 53, to watch the life in natural conditions under the rocks without putting your head under water. It would help this study still more to put underwater a pail or box with a sealed glass bottom, so you can look at your mirror without having ripples bother your vision.

Take notes on everything you observe, and build the facts you find into a synthesis that has real meaning. A map of the stream to show where each kind of life is found would be most useful, as would graphs to show the fluctuation and the rhythm of life in relation to stream flow, temperature, light and darkness, and so on. (Figure 54.)

(4) Study selected water life in an aquarium. You

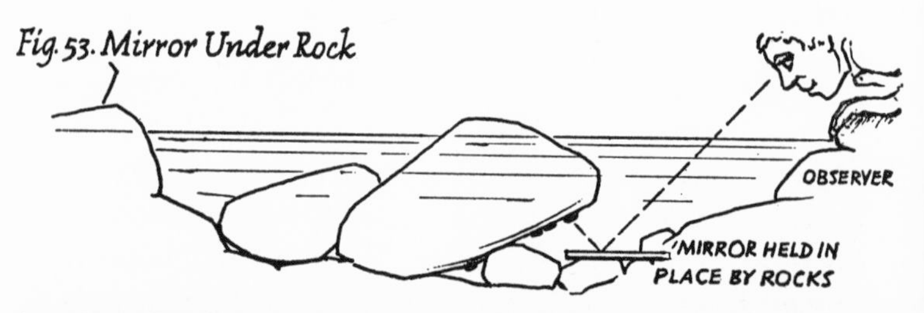

Fig. 53. Mirror Under Rock

MIRROR IS EFFECTIVE IN STILL OR SLOW-MOVING WATER, BUT IMAGE IS DISTORTED BY FAST CURRENT OR WAVE MOTION. SUN SHOULD NOT SHINE DIRECTLY ON MIRROR. IF A MAGNIFYING CONCAVE MIRROR IS USED, IT MUST BE FOCUSED CAREFULLY WHEN PUT IN PLACE. WATER MUST BE CLEAR TO BE SEEN THROUGH.

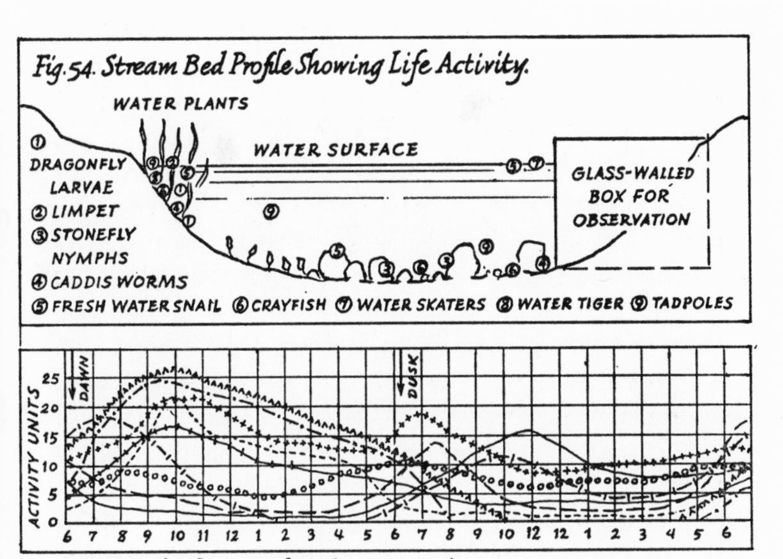

Fig. 54. Stream Bed Profile Showing Life Activity.

Fig. 54B. Graph of Day and Night Stream Activity ①--- ②— ③— ④---- ⑤oooooo ⑥+++++ ⑦-·-·. ⑧-ı-ı- ⑨ ^^^^ (NOTE: GRAPH IS IMAGINARY, BASED ON EXPERIENCE BUT NOT ACTUAL RECORDS)

should have a balanced aquarium, and one which duplicates as closely as possible natural surroundings of the animals you have in it. Study the water life in a pond and try, as much as possible, to have the same things in your aquarium. (How to balance an aquarium, collect animals and plants for it, and take care of them, are all fully explained in my book, *How to Make a Miniature Zoo*). Maps, diagrams and graphs, such as those already shown to you in this book, could be used to record your observations of life in your aquarium in a systematic way. You can also experiment with new life introduced to the aquarium, and also test the reactions of your aquarium animals to various chemicals put in their water. However, be careful to not treat your animals cruelly. Keep separate notes on each species of life in your aquarium, building up your knowledge of them until you begin to study new things about them no man has seen before.

(5) Explore the effect of wave action on life of a rocky shore, watching this action at stated intervals and recording all changes noted. Animal and plant life along a seashore is strongly influenced by the ebb and flow of the tide, bringing food and moisture from the sea, but it is also influenced by the power of the waves that beat upon the shore. Every living thing along the shore must find ways to protect itself against wave action, particularly the great storm waves that sometimes hurl whole boulders against them. Some life builds strong armor, as the hard-shelled barnacles do, that protects it against the blows of the sea. Other kinds, such as the plant seaweed and the sea-feathers, move with the waves, back and forth, without resisting them. Still other forms, such as sea anemones and the sea urchins, seek for or build hollows in the rocks which will protect their bodies. A fourth kind of life, such as Nereis worms and tiny amphipods and crabs, lives in crevices among the shells of the armored mussels or barnacles. A fifth kind are the seashells, like piddock clams, that actually bore into the rocks, thus avoiding completely the blow of the waves.

But a close watch is needed to see just how these creatures act to get the greatest possible protection when the great waves come. For this exploration you need to first map a rock face near the sea at very low tide, showing where all the different animals and plants are found (Figure 55). A photograph would also be helpful. The rock face should then be carefully watched again at each low tide and particularly after a storm, mapping any changes in the locations of animals and plants or their destruction by the waves (Figure 56).

This adventure — and it would surely be a great adventure! — might lead to much new knowledge about wave action on life. It might be necessary to build some kind of wave gauge, an instrument that would measure

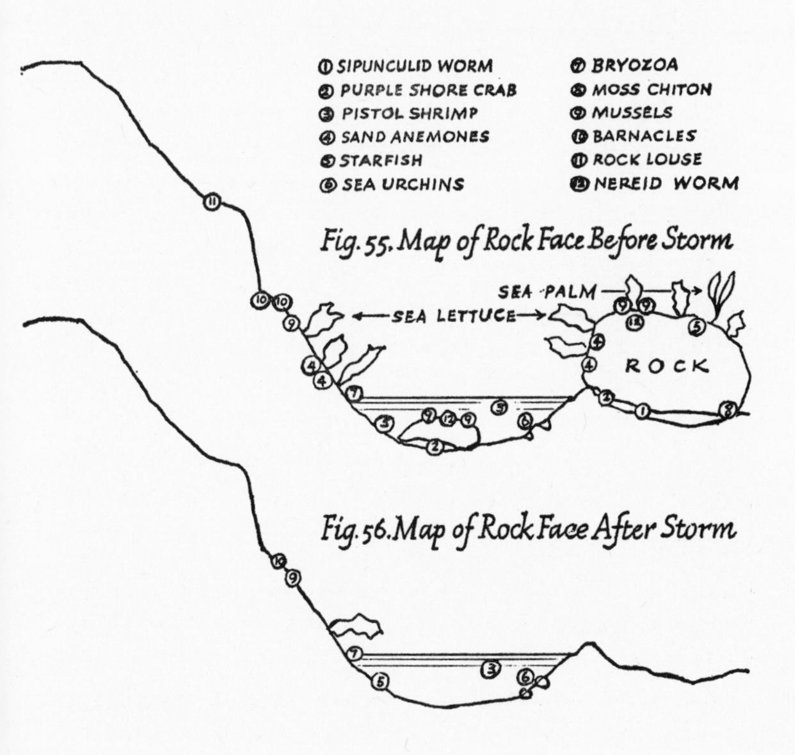

Fig. 55. Map of Rock Face Before Storm

Fig. 56. Map of Rock Face After Storm

the force in pounds pressure per foot or inch of each wave that came in. Ask at the marine biology department of your nearest university about such an instrument. A graph would show animals and plants killed, torn loose or otherwise injured by each wave (Figure 57). At the same time you would take notes to show how different animals withstood the heavy wave action.

(6) Explore the hidden worlds of a kelp bed. Along our shores in the ocean lie great beds of kelp, some of them stretching for hundreds of yards. In the thick and almost impenetrable jungle of such a kelp bed live myriad forms of life that find there protections against both the waves of the sea and the large and fierce creatures that hunt in the sea. In the Pacific Ocean, the sea otter likes to hide from its enemies, the sharks and killer

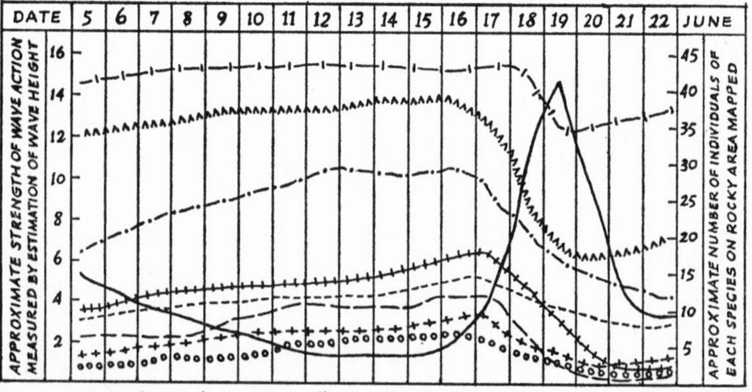

Fig. 57. Graph of the Action of Waves on Animals

WAVE HEIGHT — SIPUNCULID WORMS —— SHORE CRABS +++ SHRIMPS ooooo ANEMONES —·—· STARFISH ---- CHITONS +·+·+ MUSSELS ʌʌʌʌ BARNACLES —ı—ı—

whales, in these beds. It finds them wonderfully safe nurseries for its children as well as places to hunt for food such as mussels, clams and other seashells.

There are two ways to study the kelp bed's life, but they should be combined if possible. One way is to go out to the bed in a boat, taking along a glass-bottomed pail on a calm day. Through the pail you study the life of the surface of the kelp bed; perhaps you will also climb out and walk around on the surface of the bed (or swim) in order to watch and collect things. The second way is to become a skin-diver, so that you can swim under the bed and study the life on the underside. Since there is risk in being a skin diver, you should definitely join a skin-diving organization so that you can do your skin-diving in coöperation with and under the watchful eye of those experienced enough to come to your rescue in case of trouble, divers who would make sure that you did not take foolish chances.

The kelp bed you study should be mapped. On this map you can then chart out where different types of animal and plant life are found. This may require a three-dimensional map, or even a three-dimensional model, so that it can be seen exactly where different things are found (Figure 58). Your exploration will show how different sorts of life choose different kinds of places to live in the bed and how they gather food and protect themselves from enemies. In some places you may even find social animals who communicate with one another, and a study of this communication will reveal a secret world in itself. For instance the sea otters, who dwell in kelp beds, have a very wide range of communication, be-

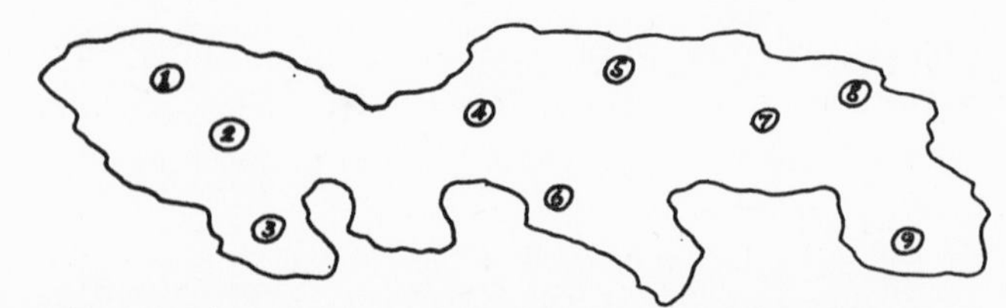

Fig. 58. Plan (ABOVE) and vertical section (BELOW) of Kelp Bed.
ANIMALS FOUND AT DIFFERENT POINTS ARE LISTED UNDER A NUMBER (SURFACE) OR A LETTER (BELOW SURFACE)

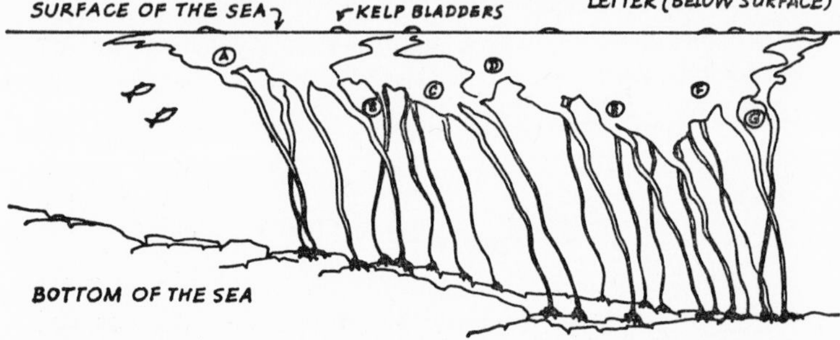

ing perhaps the most intelligent and humanlike animals of the sea.

(7) Explore the hidden worlds of a mud flat. In almost any bay or estuary there are usually extensive mud flats and salt-water marshes, where most of the life is hidden. To find and understand this life, you must walk out into a flat at low tide and dig down through its mud. Notice that the sorts of life are quite different at different tide levels, but all are dependent on the tide bringing in food in the form of tiny plankton from the sea. How the life of the mud flat captures its food is an adventure story. The "fat innkeeper" (a polychaete worm), builds a net in its burrow out of its own saliva and catches in this net the tiny life the sea brings in at high tide. But in-

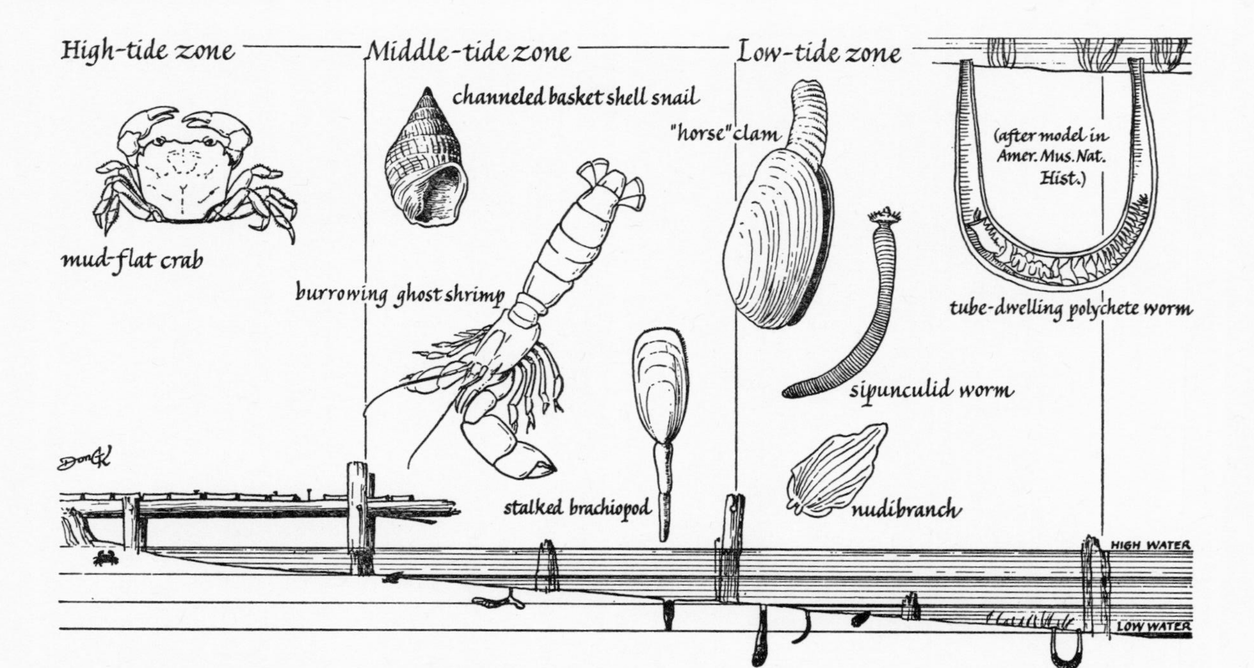

FIG. 59 Forms of life at various tide levels of a mud-flat of sheltered bay or estuary.

Animals not to relative scale.
After Ricketts and others.

side the inn (or tunnel) of the innkeeper, other creatures — such as a tiny crab, a fish, and a shield worm — live as guests and eat also from that dinner table.

The old way to find out these secrets of the mud flat was simply to dig down through the mud and uncover the various clams, ghost shrimps and other creatures that are found there. But you can invent new ways that may show you the under-mud life under more natural conditions. For example, you could push a glass bucket down into the mud and watch the life you could see through the sides and bottom of the bucket. Or a more elaborate glass-sided box could be pushed down into the mud so that you could actually watch the animal life in a natural way. (Figure 60.) With this type of device, you could watch how the mud flat animals feed on the tiny life the tide brings in and on each other. If studies could also be made at night with a red light so as not to disturb the animals, even more revealing insights into the lives of the queer, mud flat animals might be discovered. A large magnifying glass to watch their feeding would probably be very helpful for this job.

It is possible also to try to reproduce mud flat conditions in your own home aquarium, providing you can learn to supply the mud flat animals you have captured with the kind of food they want. Then, through the glass sides of the aquarium, which you would need to keep covered with dark cloth except when opened for observation, you would watch methods of feeding and hiding. Naturally this could never be quite as good as in the mud flat itself.

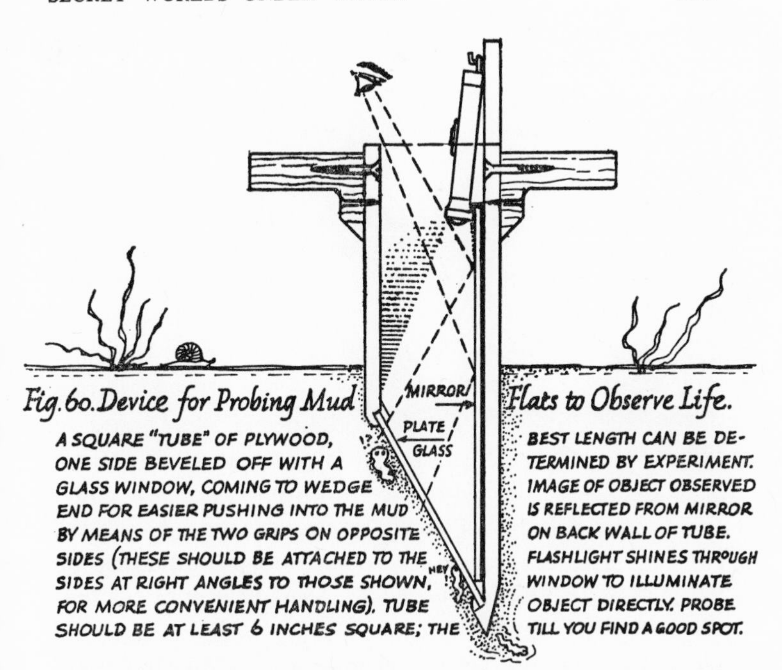

Fig. 60. Device for Probing Mud Flats to Observe Life.

A SQUARE "TUBE" OF PLYWOOD, ONE SIDE BEVELED OFF WITH A GLASS WINDOW, COMING TO WEDGE END FOR EASIER PUSHING INTO THE MUD BY MEANS OF THE TWO GRIPS ON OPPOSITE SIDES (THESE SHOULD BE ATTACHED TO THE SIDES AT RIGHT ANGLES TO THOSE SHOWN, FOR MORE CONVENIENT HANDLING). TUBE SHOULD BE AT LEAST 6 INCHES SQUARE; THE BEST LENGTH CAN BE DETERMINED BY EXPERIMENT. IMAGE OF OBJECT OBSERVED IS REFLECTED FROM MIRROR ON BACK WALL OF TUBE. FLASHLIGHT SHINES THROUGH WINDOW TO ILLUMINATE OBJECT DIRECTLY. PROBE TILL YOU FIND A GOOD SPOT.

In both cases maps and graphs will help you build your conclusions or syntheses from the facts you gather. A map in three dimensions shows where the animals are found. Graphs show what times they feed in relation to the coming of the tide, and on what they feed.

(8) A very similar study can be made of life in a tide pool among the rocks of a seashore or of life in the sand of a sandy beach. Any way you can find to get beneath the surfaces of these places and see the life moving and living in natural conditions will make your exploration of these secret worlds richer and more meaningful.

8

SECRET WORLDS OF THE SKY

OVER US all is the changing sky. Clouds of infinite variety and form move across it and even when it is clear the vast oceans of air are shifting above us, moving the smog that rises from our cities so that the citizens can breathe, or sometimes trapping the foul air until people become sick or even die. Into the sky man sends out searching fingers and eyes in the form of balloons, rockets, telescopes, and other tools of exploration. More and more facts are found each year to add to our knowledge of weather and climate, to help the farmer guard our industries, and help us fight insects and other enemies. This is another kind of exploration that has just begun, and you too can join in the great search for the secrets of the sky.

Perhaps the best way to start your search is to visit a local weather station, observe the uses of their instruments, charts, maps and graphs, and ask questions. From this you move on to a study of books about the weather and climate. Particularly you should become familiar with the different main types of cloud formations, the cumulus, cumulo-nimbus, cirrus and stratus clouds, and their effects on weather and climate. Study the rules of wind force, and the way rain, snow, hail and lightning are made. Good books giving full information on these subjects are listed in the back of this book. My *Amateur Naturalist's Handbook* gives many details on weather and climate.

It is particularly necessary to understand the great air masses that move over the northern hemisphere, changing the weather as they come, particularly along the borders where air mass meets air mass. Also of vital interest are the laws governing the formation of storms.

From these studies you will begin to see what particular explorations of the sky you would like to make. But here are some suggestions:

(1) If you live in or near a desert, you have a wonderful opportunity to watch one of the strangest of all natural phenomena, the carving of rocks by desert winds and the effect of these winds on desert life and soil. You will first need to study the laws of wind force and to build two instruments, a wind direction indicator and a wind gauge (Figure 61). The wind indicator helps you mark down from hour to hour the wind direction at each of your observation stations. The wind gauge shows you the actual force of the wind, which may vary from a force of 0 (absolute calm on the Beaufort Scale of Wind Force) to a force of 12 (a hurricane wind of over seventy-five miles an hour on the same scale).

Over a period of several weeks or months or even years you can build up a vast number of vital facts about the effect of wind force in a particular section of desert

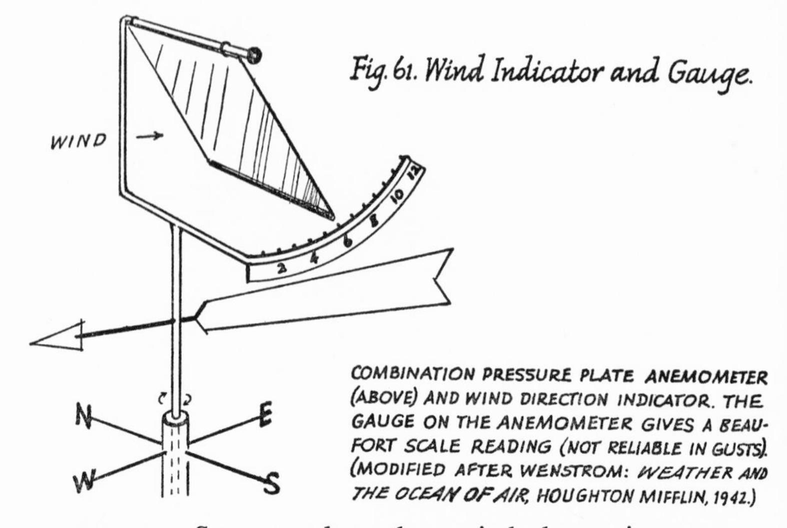

Fig. 61. Wind Indicator and Gauge.

COMBINATION PRESSURE PLATE ANEMOMETER (ABOVE) AND WIND DIRECTION INDICATOR. THE GAUGE ON THE ANEMOMETER GIVES A BEAUFORT SCALE READING (NOT RELIABLE IN GUSTS). (MODIFIED AFTER WENSTROM: *WEATHER AND THE OCEAN OF AIR*, HOUGHTON MIFFLIN, 1942.)

near you. Set out at least three wind observation posts, more if you can arrange it, and visit each post at least twice a day. Write down in your notebook the exact time you visit each post. At the post, record the direction of the wind, the wind force, and anything you can see about the effect of the wind on rocks, soil or plants. At least one of your observation posts should be right next to a rock pinnacle or other rock formation that is being shaped by the wind and the dust it brings. To watch the erosion of such rock under the scouring of a high wind, you will probably need to build a small, sheltered observation post with a window so that you can stay there and watch even in the highest winds. (Figure 62.)

I have been on the desert in a wind force of 9, which means forty-seven to fifty-four miles per hour, and seen the grit and dust carried by the wind actually strip the

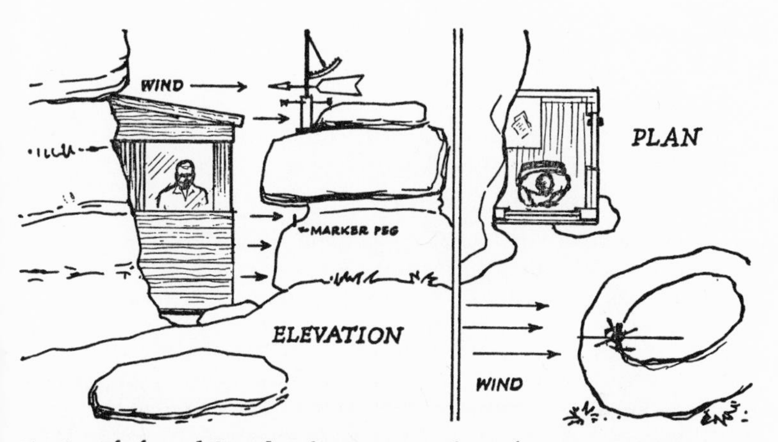

Fig. 62. Sheltered Post for Observation of Wind Erosion on Rock.
THE STRUCTURE AND ORIENTATION OF SUCH A POST WILL OF COURSE DEPEND ON THE NATURE OF THE SITE. THE WINDOW MUST BE PROTECTED FROM THE DIRECT FORCE OF THE SAND-LADEN WIND, WHICH CUTS BACK THE SOFTER LAYERS OF SEDIMENTARY ROCKS FAST ENOUGH TO BE MEASURED.

paint off the body of a car. In this wind you could see the sandpaper-like action of the fine dust eating into the side of a soft sandstone rock at the rate of about a sixteenth of an inch an hour. It is easy to see how the strange and fantastic rock formations found in desert regions were formed. But much more information is needed about how and when the wind does this, which is why it would be such an interesting exploration.

(2) Explore the great air masses to understand their taste, feeling and smell, and the emotions they bring to men. The ocean of air above us changes gradually throughout the year as one air mass supplants another. In the heart of the North American continent occur such air masses as the Polar Canadian, the Tropical Gulf,

occasionally the Polar Atlantic and the Tropical Continental, and very rarely the excessively dry Sec Superieur. On the Pacific Coast the Polar Pacific of the rainy winters and springs struggles back and forth with the Tropical Pacific air mass of the dry summers and falls. Each of these air masses has a particular taste, feeling and smell and also affects the emotions of men in different ways. How it does so is still a study in its infancy, and there is much more to learn.

You can take part in this exploration by keeping careful records of human reactions, including your own, during the time each of the great air masses is present, and also during the time when your area is in the border between two such giants struggling for mastery. All border struggles usually show signs of upset in the climate, with wild swings between extremes of storm and calm within a comparatively few hours. At such times the emotions of men are possibly most upset by the weather. But careful research, is necessary in order to learn the truth about the effect of air masses on human emotions.

First you need to be sure through study and research that you can recognize each of the great air masses when it comes and also when you are in the border country between air masses. Then you need to keep careful records of human emotional reactions in your area during each of these periods. You can get much information from the newspapers, also from the records of police stations, for certain crimes seem to be committed more in certain types of weather. Another thing to watch for is your own feelings and emotions during these air-mass

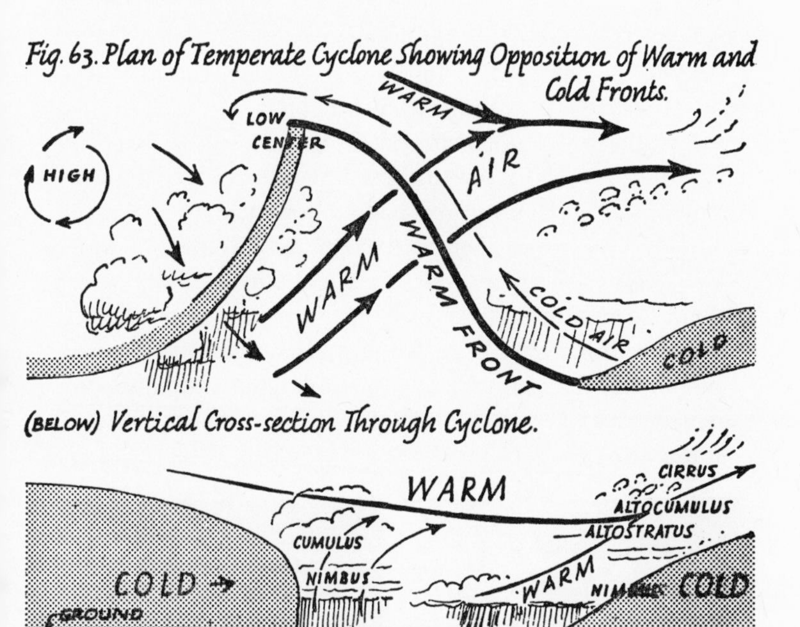

Fig. 63. Plan of Temperate Cyclone Showing Opposition of Warm and Cold Fronts.

(BELOW) Vertical Cross-section Through Cyclone.

periods and the feelings and emotions of your friends. Record from day to day every fact of such nature you observe or otherwise find. It is the building up of many such tiny facts that finally brings you to the truth.

(3) Explore unusual cloud formations and their meanings. Every so often you see in the sky some cloud formation of unusual beauty or strangeness. Something has caused the clouds to form in this way. What is it and how does it act? First write down the exact time you see a strange cloud formation and how long it lasts, what part of the sky it is in, all changes of color and appear-

ance that you see. Be careful to leave out nothing that you notice. Even a tiny fact may help give you a clue to the reason for this strange thing you have seen.

After all these notes are taken, make a series of paintings or maps of the sky to show how the cloud formation changed. Of course, if you have a good camera, pictures of the sky can be taken at five- or ten-minute intervals. (Figure 64.) Show your local weather station your cloud-formation pictures or maps, and tell them all that you have observed. Ask them what they think has caused this cloud formation, but do not take their explanations as necessarily being completely true. Use their explanation as one you will have to investigate, but try to think

Fig. 64. Movement and Change in Cumulo-nimbus Rain Cloud.

PHOTOS TAKEN 5 MINUTES APART OF LINE SQUALL PASSING EASTWARD OVER ISLAND 3.5 MILES AWAY. CLEAR BLUE SKY ABOVE, DISTANT CLOUDS BELOW. THE SOLID-LOOKING CUMULUS HOLDS GENERAL SHAPE WHILE SLOWLY EVOLVING AS ITS MASS TRAVELS WITH THE WIND, DUMPING HEAVY RAIN FROM ITS NEARLY FLAT BOTTOM. ARROWS SHOW MOVEMENT OF BILLOWS. (PHOTOS TAKEN IN MARCH ON SAN FRANCISCO BAY BY D.G.K.)

of as many other explanations as you can. This is the scientific method and means you investigate all possibilities about the cause of a natural phenomena with equal care and equal lack of prejudice.

Ask your nearby weather station to let you see their maps and any photos or other data they have about the weather at the particular time of the day you saw the strange formation. Perhaps it was caused by a change in the weather pattern at that time. Visit nearby universities or colleges where there are weather experts and ask them their opinions and for any facts they have available about the cloud formation that day. Store all such information in your notebook.

The unscientific explorer would be satisfied with one such observation and one such visit to the weather station. He would accept their explanation of what happened and let it go at that. But, if you are a true explorer, you will continue your study of strange cloud formations for many months and perhaps for years before you can finally come up with some real conclusions that hold up under investigation about what has happened in the sky and why and how. Over a period of months, for example, you would notice that one particular kind of cloud formation occurred five times. If the same kind of humidity, wind force and direction, temperature and cloudiness appeared at each of these times, you would begin to see what things caused that particular cloud formation. But, if the weather conditions varied, then you would seek for a different reason — perhaps the influence of heavy outpourings of smoke from a city, or the effect of a particular wind from the sea.

(4) Explore the laws of motion and building among cumulus clouds. Cumulus clouds, the big fluffy white clouds that look like sheep in the sky or sometimes like towering castles, are moved both by horizontal winds and by updrafts of air from the ground. They appear most often in fairly warm weather, when the heated air near the surface of the ground rises into the sky. This rising air current pushes up the clouds and also helps build them larger, often turning them in the course of a day from ordinary cumulus clouds to the huge and ominous thunderheads of cumulo-nimbus.

This sort of exploration requires numerous observations of the cumulus clouds in action, and careful notes of all you observe. Each observation needs to be accompanied by a written record of both wind speed and direction at that particular time, as well as some indication of the speed of updraft from the ground; measure also if possible the size of each cumulus cloud from hour to hour, its direction and speed of motion. Add any other facts you can observe. If the shadow of the cloud passes near by, you can often race along with it and make a fairly accurate judge of its speed, since the average man runs at full speed at about fifteen miles an hour. Of course, if you can drive a car or motorcycle along just in front of the shadow, you can determine more accurately its speed.

Kites, or better yet balloons, can be sent up into the sky on the end of long strings to bring down information about the cumulus clouds. The way the balloon drifts and the amount of pull it exerts on the string help you determine wind speed and direction high in the sky. If you can send up with the balloon or kite instruments such as a wind-gauge, thermometer, humidity indicator, you will need also to have some way of obtaining the records they show. Visit your local weather station and ask for details before trying this.

WARNING: Do not send either kites or balloons up into a cumulo-nimbus cloud, as you may get a bad electric shock!

Photography of the sky every ten minutes or at some other regular interval will show how the clouds change

DATE	MAY 2	MAY 3	MAY 4	MAY 5	MAY 6
TYPE OF CLOUDS	ALTO-CUMULUS	CIRRUS	CIRRO-STRATUS	ALTO-STRATUS	NIMBO-STRATUS
TEMPERATURE: 7 A.M.	47° F	45°	49°	48°	55°
1 P.M.	55°	52°	56°	55°	60°
WIND VELOCITY	10 MPH	12	15	20	35
WIND DIRECTION	DUE E	ENE	NE	N	NW
HUMIDITY: PER CENT	49	55	70	85	100
BAROMETRIC PRESSURE	30.7	30.5	30.1	29.8	29.3
SUNLIGHT: PERCENT	90	85	50	40	5
RAINFALL	0	0	0	0	1.2 IN.
DIRECTION CLOUDS MOVING	DUE E	DUE E	DUE E	NE	NE

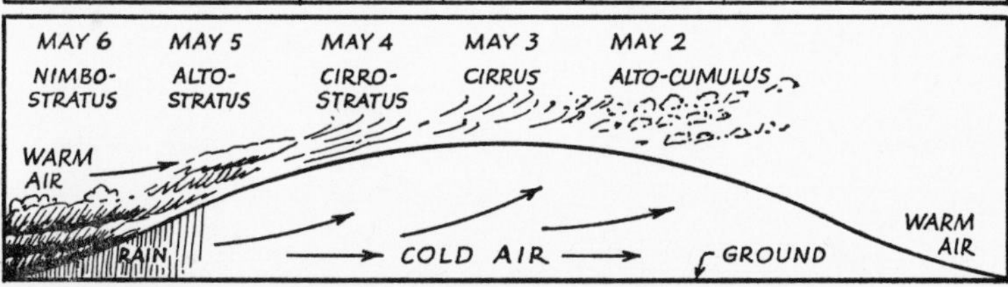

Fig. 65. Relation of Clouds to Other Weather Phenomena.

GRAPH (ABOVE) SYNCHRONIZES WITH CROSS-SECTION (BELOW) OF WEATHER DEPRESSION (AFTER KENDREW: *WEATHER*, OXFORD, 1953). WEATHER FRONT MOVING FROM LEFT TO RIGHT. TIME MOVING FROM RIGHT TO LEFT.

and move. To go with these photos you will make graphs to show how variations in temperature, humidity, wind speed and so on have influenced the movement of the clouds. (Figure 65.) Perhaps you can get such records from your nearest weather station, for the same days that you were taking observations. By combining and synthesizing all these facts, you will begin to get a picture of the laws that govern the movement and building of cumulus clouds.

9

SECRET WORLDS OF OUTER SPACE

OUTER SPACE is now being explored by rocket ships, satellites and other methods that cost into the many millions of dollars. You might ask, "What could I do to explore outer space when I have very little money?" It is perfectly true that you can do little or nothing yourself to explore outer space in the big way of the rocket ships and satellites or the great telescopes. But there are small ways to explore, and the secret of success in these small ways is to specialize. You need to specialize in some small facet of astronomy or astrophysics about which little is known, and combine your specialized knowledge with those of other small observers into something that can often be of great importance. For example, you can join one of the organizations of amateur star and planet observers that are formed all over the world to carry on specialized work of this kind, adding every year to astronomical knowledge.

Actually, if you live not very far away from a large astronomical observatory and show your interest and knowledge by the questions you ask when you visit it, and if you are careful to be modest and courteous in every action and word, you may find yourself invited some night to join the astonomers in their observations. Some day you may even be permitted to use one of the great telescopes part of the time, as a qualified amateur astonomer whom the professionals have decided might be of help to them in finding out more about the secrets of the skies.

Another possibility is to form an astronomical club and build a telescope of sufficient power to explore the skies. Kits for making such telescopes are sold through advertisements in science magazines. Be sure to get one of good quality — ask an astronomer you know for advice, if possible. You can probably make a good six-inch reflecting telescope with magnifications up to at least 250 diameters for less than seventy-five dollars. Get at least a six-inch reflector, because the smaller sizes cannot reach the magnification necessary for really scientific star and planet study.

If you live in a city where there is much smog, you may have to drive with your telescope to the top of some high hill or mountain where the atmosphere is clear. It is necessary, of course, to have a good tripod with a swinging pivot so the telescope can be swung easily in any direction.

Here are some suggested secret worlds of outer space to explore:

(1) Study the variations in the appearance of the atmosphere of Venus, with research into the laws and cycles these changes might reflect. To do a job of this complexity you would need to work in close coöperation

with your nearest observatory and also correspond with observers and observatories in other parts of the world. But first of all you would need to study every bit of literature you could find on this subject. In the library of almost any big observatory such literature can be found. Look in the indexes of the books and find every reference you can on the subject. Write down this information in your notebook. If your notebook has loose-leaf pages, you can later arrange such notes in a systematic way so that every fact is where you can easily find it.

Begin your observations of Venus through your own telescope, being sure that changes you see in the appearance of the atmosphere of Venus are not due to changes in the earth's atmosphere. It is best, of course, to make your observations from as high an altitude as possible, so the atmosphere of the earth will not get too much in your way. Each time you note a change in the appearance of the atmosphere of Venus, note the change in your notebook. If you can catch this change photographically through your telescope, that would be much better. Note the exact date, hour and minute when each such observation and photo is made. The best of all times to photograph Venus is when its shape is like that of a half moon. At such times, the atmosphere of Venus is lit up more by the light of the sun, and so more of it can be seen. (Figure 66.)

Your own photos and drawings are, of course, only a small part of the study you must do in this exploration. You need to study every single photograph of Venus that is reproduced in books and every one you can get to see at your nearest observatory. Take notes on every slight

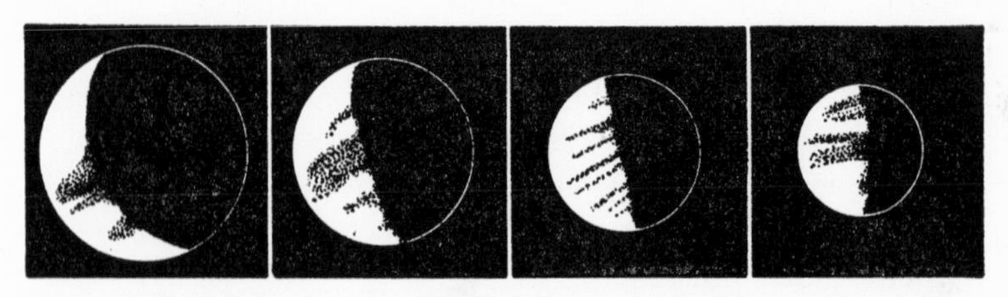

Fig. 66. Venus and its Atmosphere Seen in Different Phases.

VENUS IS NEARER THE SUN THAN THE EARTH IS. THESE DRAWINGS (AFTER R.S. RICHARDSON, MT. WILSON AND PALOMAR OBSERVATORIES) SHOW IT—FROM LEFT TO RIGHT—PROGRESSIVELY FARTHER FROM EARTH. IT IS BRIGHTEST WHEN IT IS CLOSEST, EVEN THOUGH LESS OF ITS SURFACE IS RECEIVING SUNLIGHT. DARK AREAS IN THE CLOUD COVER ARE CONSTANTLY CHANGING.

APRIL 7

APRIL 9

APRIL 11

Fig. 67. Diagram Recording Observations of Shifting Spot on Venus.

variation in the atmosphere that you observe in these pictures. If you can, visit other observatories and study their photos of Venus, but often your neighborhood observatory will have copies of photos taken at other observatories. As each photo is studied, write about it in your notebook, noting any unusual features you observe (as shown in Figure 67), eventually putting these facts into a graph) that reveals meaningful laws and cycles of changes about the atmosphere of Venus. Whether what you discover will be new to astronomers is up to them to judge.

(2) Explore the changing aspects of a certain section

of night sky which you watch night after night through your telescope. If all the telescopes, small and large, at present in the world, were focused at the same moment on the night sky, it is unlikely they could cover even half. This makes it very possible for you to watch a certain section that other astronomers are not watching. By inspecting it carefully night after night, you may make a discovery of great importance — such as the coming of a new comet toward the earth, or a new planetoid, or a nova or exploding star, or even a new variable star. Any one of these discoveries would be a great aid to science.

The best way to do this job is to go to your nearest observatory or university and ask them what part of the sky they would suggest for your work — a part that, so far as they know, nobody else is studying. Get the correct azimuthal reading (you can find out about this in any good book on astronomy) of your section of the sky; then center your telescope on it and keep it there. Your telescope will either have to be moved with your hand to keep it focused on the right spot in the sky as the earth turns, or, better yet, you can obtain a clockwork attachment that will keep the telescope always pointed at the same spot in the sky.

Your first job is either to make a photograph of your sky section or draw an accurate map of it. The photograph is best, and you should have your camera ready to take another photograph through the telescope whenever it appears necessary. Study both your photograph (or map) and your section of the sky through the telescope most carefully until you are sure you know every detail. (Figure 68.) From a large sky map at an observatory,

Fig. 68. Photograph of a Portion of the Sky.

DISTANT CLUSTER OF GALAXIES IN THE CONSTELLATION COMA BERENICES. OVER 30,000,000 LIGHT YEARS AWAY. BEAN-SHAPED OBJECT IS TWO COLLIDING GALAXIES. (PHOTOGRAPH COURTESY OF MOUNT WILSON-PALOMAR OBSERVATORIES)

with which you can compare your photograph or map, find out the correct name of each star or nebula that appears in your sky section. Familiarize yourself with these names so the instant any change occurs you can give an intelligent and accurate report of the exact place it happened.

Patience and careful watching night after night are now the main requirements of your exploration. Watch for the slightest change in your portion of the sky. For days, weeks, even months or years, nothing may happen. Then suddenly a new star or nova appears, or a new asteroid swims into sight, or you see the beginning of a new comet. On that exciting night it is to be hoped that you will have at least one other person working with you, or one whom you can call right away from a nearby telephone. Immediately start photographing this new object you have discovered and keep photographing it every few minutes, as quite remarkable changes may appear. One of you should immediately phone the nearest observatory, giving your name and address, the azimuthal reading or measurement, and the exact nature of what you have seen. Keep careful notes of all the changes you notice. Those notes, if done rightly, may later be of incalculable value.

(3) If you can attach a spectroscope to your telescope, you can analyze the lights from different stars and explore many aspects of star nature that the telescope alone cannot do. The spectroscope shows you the chemical elements of which a star is made, and also may give you a key to its distance from the earth and its relation to any dark bodies that pass around it. There are what are called spectroscopic variable stars whose variations in light can only be detected and understood with the spectroscope.

How to use a spectroscope is a subject you need to study in a good modern astronomy book such as one of those listed in the end of this book. A visit to your local observatory may lead the astronomer there to give you a demonstration of the use of the spectroscope if you ask him courteously to do so.

If you do obtain a spectroscope to attach to your telescope, again you should specialize. As in the exploration described before this one, select a particular section of the sky that has been little or not at all studied and spectroscopically analyze each of the stars and nebulae that are found in that area. (Figure 69.) Such spectroscopic analysis is not to be done by a beginner, but only after careful study and training. First, study all you can about it in books; then practice either with a spectroscope attached to your own telescope or by work at one of the great observatories. Make analyses of the spectra of different stars from your study of the spectroscopic lines on each spectrum and take your analyses to an astronomer who has offered to check your findings. Your analyses should become more and more accurate.

When you have analyzed with a spectroscope all the spectra of stars in the particular section of the sky you are studying, you are ready to find out what the analyses tell about the nature of the stars. Take your findings to an expert and get his opinion. Find out also, through research and study, what changes in spectra may mean. This is important, because as often as possible you will need to repeat your spectrum analyses of the different

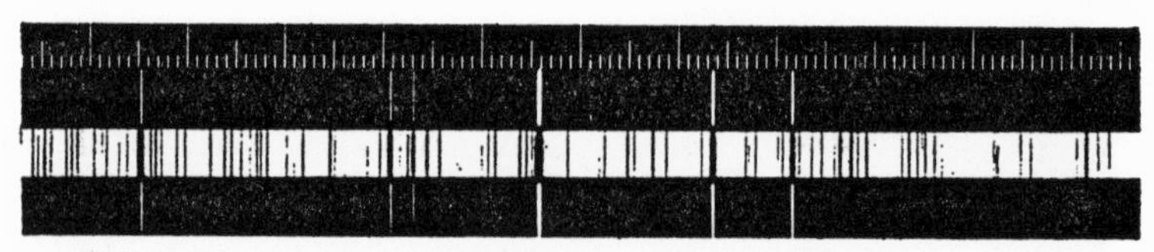

Fig. 69. A Star Spectrum (Light Strip in the Middle) and Analysis.

SUPERIMPOSED ON IRON SPECTRUM, ITS HEAVY DARK LINES MATCHING, SHOW THERE IS IRON IN THE STAR. OTHER LINES INDICATE OTHER ELEMENTS. (FROM *THE WORLD OF SCIENCE*, BY JANE WERNER WATSON, SIMON AND SCHUSTER, NEW YORK, 1958.)

stars in your study area of the sky to see if any spectra have changed in character. Certain changes may show the presence of a dark body circling the glowing star. This could be an exciting discovery of a spectroscopic variable star. Other changes may help show how far away the star is from the earth, whether it is partly circled by a gaseous nebula, whether it is variable because of some kind of pulsating change in the chemical nature of the star, and whether it might be getting ready to explode.

Every change must be carefully noted and photographed. Report these changes to your astronomer friend and follow his directions as to what to do. By continuing to keep careful records and to make accurate photographs you will finally build up enough facts and knowledge to come to some useful conclusions about what is happening in your section of the sky. Sometimes you can even prophesy what is going to happen there — such as the sudden appearance of a new nova, an exploding star.

(4) There are many special little problems that astronomers face in their study of the universe or of distant nebulae. And sometimes what seems to be a little problem can lead to a very big discovery. Only when you have become very well acquainted with professional astronomers and have shown them that your interest is genuine should you ask them to suggest to you a problem for you to explore. The exploration might be of the giant red stars, like Antares and Betelgeuse, that are more enormous by thousands of times than our own sun. There might be some unique reason for the place these stars occupy in our universe if we could find out a relationship

between their exact locations and those of other kinds of stars.

Another problem could be worked out by studying one particular variable star and watching it constantly over a period of months to see what causes it to be variable. If you constantly photographed this star and took its spectrum at regular intervals for a while, and then at irregular intervals — all carefully marked on a chart or graph — you might finally catch the secret of the star's nature, a secret worthy of any scientific explorer.

Fig. 70. A Scientific Discovery.

THREE "ARDENT AMATEUR PALEONTOLOGISTS"-AGE 16 AND 17-UNLOCKED ONE OF NATURE'S BEST KEPT SECRETS WHEN THEY FOUND IN A NEW JERSEY QUARRY A FOSSIL OF A SOARING REPTILE,"THOUGT TO BE FIRST VERTEBRATE TO TAKE TO THE AIR"-THE *NEW YORK TIMES* REPORTED. THIS FIND WAS OF ENORMOUS IMPORTANCE TO SCIENCE BECAUSE IT WAS "THE ONLY ONE OF ITS KIND YET FOUND" AT THAT TIME. (FOSSIL AT RIGHT SKETCHED FROM PHOTOGRAPH IN *DISCOVERIES IN ANCIENT LIFE* BY VINSON BROWN, SCIENCE MATERIALS CENTER, INC., 59 FOURTH AVENUE, NEW YORK 3, NEW YORK. ©1961.)

(5) Other instruments that can help you penetrate secret worlds in outer space include a gauge for measuring cosmic rays, a telescope specially made for photographing sun spots or eclipses, and so on. Ask about these instruments and others at your nearest observatory.

Do not be misled by the glitter and glory of the first space explorers in rocket ships. Their exploration of outer space is no more important or necessary than many an exploration into the unknown you can do on earth. Inside, all true explorers have the same toughness, the will and courage and stamina to keep on seeking when others turn back. You can develop this toughness of the spirit and the mind. Turn defeats or failures into lessons about how to move on to victory. Never give up. And never stop being curious! Curiosity plus determination combine to make the explorer who will dare to undertake the great adventure of entering, finding and knowing the unknown.

The day shall not be up as soon as I,
To try the fair adventure of to-morrow.

— William Shakespeare

BIBLIOGRAPHY: SUGGESTED REFERENCES

BIBLIOGRAPHY: SUGGESTED REFERENCES

The following books are suggested sources of information in your exploration of secret worlds. These are only a few of the books you could possibly use, but they are some of the best. Other books can be found in your library or ordered through your library. (A large book, found in most libraries, called *Subject Guide to Books in Print,* lists most of the books in print under any subject title.) You should also turn to scientific magazines for information. Almost any university or college has these scientific magazines in its library.

General Natural History and Nature Study

AMATEUR NATURALIST'S HANDBOOK, by Vinson Brown. 1948. Little, Brown.

FIELD BOOK OF NATURAL HISTORY, by E. Laurence Palmer. 1949. McGraw-Hill.

HOW TO MAKE A HOME NATURE MUSEUM, by Vinson Brown. 1954. Little, Brown.

SOURCE-BOOK OF BIOLOGICAL NAMES AND TERMS, by Edmund C. Jaeger. Second Edition, 1950. Thomas. Helps with scientific names.

WORLD OF NATURAL HISTORY, John Richard Saunders. 1952. Sheridan.

WORLD OF NIGHT, by Lorus J. and Margery J. Milne. 1956. Harper.

Natural History of Special Areas

ANIMALS OF THE CANADIAN ROCKIES, by Dan McCowan. 1950. Macmillan.

BIOTIC PROVINCES OF NORTH AMERICA, by Lee R. Dice. 1943. University of Michigan.

CALIFORNIA WILDLIFE REGION, by Vinson Brown. Rev. Edit. 1957. Naturegraph.

SIERRA NEVADAN WILDLIFE REGION, by Vinson Brown. Rev. Edit. 1962. Naturegraph.

PACIFIC COASTAL WILDLIFE REGION, by Charles Yocom and Raymond Dasmann. 1957. Naturegraph.

WILD LIFE IN AMERICA, by Peter Matthiessen. 1959. Viking.

WILDLIFE OF THE INTERMOUNTAIN WEST, by Vinson Brown, Charles Yocom and Aldine Starbuck. 1958. Naturegraph.

NATURAL HISTORY OF THE SOUTHWEST, by William A. Burns. 1959. Watts.

Bacteria

GUIDE TO THE IDENTIFICATION OF THE BACTERIA, by V. B. D. Skerman. Williams and Wilkins.

Mammals

FIELD GUIDE TO THE MAMMALS, by William N. Burt and R. P. Grossenheider. 1952. Houghton Mifflin.

MAMMALS OF CALIFORNIA AND ITS COASTAL WATERS, by Lloyd G. Ingles. 1954. Stanford University Press.

MAMMALS OF NORTH AMERICA, by E. R. Hall and K. R. Kelson. 2 vols., 1959. Ronald Press Co.

Birds

FIELD GUIDE TO TEXAS BIRDS, by Roger Tory Peterson. 1960. Houghton-Mifflin.

FIELD GUIDE TO THE BIRDS, by Roger Tory Peterson. Revised edit., 1952. Houghton Mifflin. Mostly Eastern birds.

FIELD GUIDE TO WESTERN BIRDS, by Roger Tory Peterson. Rev. Edit. in 1961. Houghton Mifflin.

HANDBOOK OF CALIFORNIA BIRDS, by Vinson Brown and Henry G. Weston. 1961. Naturegraph.

Reptiles and Amphibians

AMPHIBIANS AND REPTILES OF WESTERN NORTH AMERICA, by Robert C. Stebbins. McGraw-Hill. 1954.

FIELD GUIDE TO REPTILES AND AMPHIBIANS, by Roger Conant. 1958. Houghton Mifflin. Mostly Eastern reptiles and amphibians.

Fishes

HOW TO KNOW THE FRESHWATER FISHES, by S. Eddy. 1957. W. C. Brown.

POCKET GUIDE TO THE UNDERSEA WORLD, by Ley Kenyon. 1956. Barnes.

SALT WATER FISHES FOR THE HOME AQUARIUM, by Helen Simkatis. 1957. Lippincott.

UNDERWATER NATURALIST, by Pierre De Latil. 1955. Houghton.

Insects and Their Relatives

COLLECTING, PRESERVING AND STUDYING INSECTS, by Harold Oldroyd. 1959. Macmillan.

EXPLORING THE INSECT WORLD WITH EDWIN WAY TEALE, by Edwin Way Teale. 1953. Grosset.

FIELD GUIDE TO THE BUTTERFLIES, by Alexander B. Klots. 1951. Houghton Mifflin.

HOW TO KNOW THE INSECTS, by Harry E. Jaques. 1947. W. C. Brown.

HOW TO KNOW THE BEETLES, by Harry E. Jaques. 1959. W. C. Brown.

HOW TO KNOW THE SPIDERS, by B. I. Kaston. 1959. W. C. Brown.

INSECT DIETERY: AN ACCOUNT OF THE FOOD HABITS OF INSECTS, by Charles T. Brues. 1946. Harvard University Press.

LESSER WORLDS, by Nesta Pain. 1958. Coward.

SONGS OF INSECTS, by George W. Pierce. 1948. Harvard University Press.

WONDERFUL WORLD OF INSECTS, by Albro Gaul. 1953. Rinehart.

WORLD OF BUTTERFLIES AND MOTHS, by W. B. Klots. 1958. McGraw-Hill.

Life of the Seashore

BETWEEN PACIFIC TIDES, Edward F. Ricketts and Jack Calvin. 1952. Rev. Edit. Stanford University Press.

BIOLOGY OF MARINE ANIMALS, by C. Nicol. 1959. Interscience.

FIELD BOOK OF SEASHORE LIFE, by Roy Waldo Miner. 1950. East Coast. Putnam.

FIELD GUIDE TO THE SHELLS OF OUR ATLANTIC AND GULF COASTS, by Percy A. Morris. 1951. Houghton Mifflin.

FIELD GUIDE TO THE SHELLS OF THE PACIFIC COAST AND HAWAII, by Percy A. Morris. 1952. Houghton Mifflin.

UNDERWATER GUIDE TO MARINE LIFE, by Carleton Ray and Elgin Ciampi. 1956. Barnes.

Protozoa

HOW TO KNOW THE PROTOZOA, by Theodore L. Jahn. 1949. W. C. Brown.

PROTOZOOLOGY, by Richard R. Kudo. 1954. C. C. Thomas.

Plants

CALIFORNIA FLORA, by Philip A. Munz and David D. Keck. 1959. University of California Press.

FIELD GUIDE TO THE FERNS, by Boughton Cobb. 1956. Houghton Mifflin.

FIELD GUIDE TO THE TREES AND SHRUBS, by George A. Petrides. 1958. Houghton Mifflin.

FLORA OF TEXAS, by Cyrus L. Lundell. Southern Methodist University Press.

FLORA OF THE ROCKY MOUNTAINS AND ADJACENT PLAINS, by P. A. Rydberg. 1954. Hafner.

FLORIDA WILD FLOWERS, by Mary F. Baker. 1959. Macmillan. Rev. Ed.

HOW TO KNOW THE FRESHWATER ALGAE, by Gerald W. Prescott. 1954. W. C. Brown.

HOW TO KNOW THE SEAWEEDS, by E. Yale Dawson. 1956. W. C. Brown.

HOW TO KNOW THE TREES, by Harry E. Jacques. 1946. W. C. Brown. Mainly Eastern.

HOW TO KNOW THE WESTERN TREES, by H. Baerg. 1955. W. C. Brown.

ILLUSTRATED FLORA OF THE PACIFIC STATES, by LeRoy Abrams. 4 vols. Stanford University Press.

ILLUSTRATED MANUAL OF PLANT LIFE, by R. M. Ampey. 1960. W. C. Brown.

MANUAL FOR IDENTIFICATION OF FUNGI, by Sigurd Funder. 1953. Hafner.

MANUAL OF THE SOUTHEASTERN FLORA, by Orin Alva Stevens. 1933. University of North Carolina Press.

MUSHROOM HUNTER'S FIELD GUIDE, by Alexander Smith. 1958. University of Michigan Press.

WILD FLOWERS OF AMERICA, by H. W. Rickett. 1959. Crown.

Rocks, Minerals and Fossils

FIELD GUIDE TO ROCKS AND MINERALS, by Frederick H. Pough. 1953. Houghton Mifflin.

FOSSIL BOOK, by Carroll L. and Mildred A. Fenton. 1958. Doubleday.

GETTING ACQUAINTED WITH MINERALS, by George L. English and D. E. Jensen. Rev. Ed. 1958. McGraw-Hill.

ILLUSTRATED GUIDE TO FOSSIL COLLECTING, by Richard Casanova. 1957. Naturegraph.

PLANT LIFE THROUGH THE AGES, by Albert C. Seward. 1959. Hafner.

SEARCH FOR THE PAST: An Introduction to Paleontology, by J. Beerbower. 1960. Prentice-Hall.

Astronomy

AMATEUR ASTRONOMER'S HANDBOOK, by J. B. Sidgwick. 1955. Macmillan.

ATOMS, STARS, AND NEBULAE, by L. Goldberg and L. H. Aller. 1960. Harvard University Press.

EXPLORING THE DISTANT STARS, by Clyde B. Classon. 1958. Putnam.

FIELD BOOK OF THE SKIES, by William Olcutt and others. 1954. Putnam.

Weather and Climate

ADVENTURE BOOK OF WEATHER, with kit to accompany text, by Harry Milgrom. 1959. Golden Press.

MAN, WEATHER, SUN, by William F. Petersen. 1948. C. C. Thomas.

WORKBOOK FOR WEATHER AND CLIMATE, by J. F. Lounsbury. 1959. W. C. Brown.

Microscopy

EXPLORING WITH YOUR MICROSCOPE, by Julian D. Corrington. 1957. McGraw-Hill.

WONDERS UNDER A MICROSCOPE, by Margaret Cosgrave. 1957. Dodd, Mead.

ACKNOWLEDGMENTS

Data for the chart showing the ancestry of a bean, Figure 28, by courtesy of H. M. Munger, Cornell University. After *General Genetics* by Adrian M. Srb and Ray D. Owen, W. H. Freeman and Company, San Francisco, 1952.

The bat silhouettes in Figure 29 are adapted from *Complete Field Guide to American Wildlife* by Henry Hill Collins, Jr. Copyright © 1959 by Henry Hill Collins, Jr. Reprinted by permission of Harper & Brothers.

The island family of birds in Figure 31 has been adapted from the drawing by Keulemanns in *Darwin's Finches,* by David Lack, with the permission of the Syndics of the University Press, Cambridge, England.

The maps of the Spanish Cave in Figure 45 have been adapted by permission of John Streich from a photograph by Mr. Streich in *Adventure Is Underground* by William R. Halliday.

The chart of a fossil bed, Figure 49, has been modified from *The Doubleday Pictorial Library of Nature* by permission of Rathbone Books, Ltd.

The wind indicator and gauge in Figure 61 has been modified from Wenstrom, *Weather and the Ocean of Air,* by permission of Houghton Mifflin Company.

The fossil drawing in Figure 70 was made from a photograph in *Discoveries in Ancient Life* by Vinson Brown, copyright © 1961 by Science Materials Center. Used by permission of Science Materials Center.

INDEX